A Widow's Guide To Coping With Grief: Recover From Loss, Find Happiness Again, And Rebuild Your Life!

Fiona Bishop

CONTENT

Introduction...5

Chapter 1: Introduction to grief and the grieving process 7

What is Grief...7

The importance of acknowledging and accepting grief................. 18

The role of culture and societal expectations in grief 22

Chapter 2: Effects of Grief 24

Physical.. 24

Emotional Effects 33

The importance of allowing oneself to feel and express emotions 36

Chapter 3: Finding support from friends and family 39

How to communicate your needs to loved ones 42

Exploring alternative sources of support, such as therapy or support groups.. 44

Chapter 4: Exploring different coping mechanisms......................... 47

The role of therapy in grief recovery..................................... 47

Types of therapy and how to find a therapist 51

Alternative coping mechanisms, such as journaling or art therapy 53

Chapter 5: Navigating practical tasks and responsibilities after the loss of a spouse 57

Managing finances and legal matters 57

Making Decisions about shared property and possessions 63

Adjusting to a new routine and living situation 66

Chapter 6: Finding meaning and purpose after the loss 70

Exploring new passions and interests... 70

Meeting New People 74

Finding ways to honor and remember the person who has passed
.... 79

Chapter 7: Dealing with difficult emotions..................................... 86

The importance of self-compassion and forgiveness...................... 92

Chapter 8: Moving forward and rebuilding your life......................... 95

The role of goal-setting and planning for the future...................... 100

The importance of self-discovery and personal growth 109

Chapter 9: Finding hope and happiness again.................................. 115

Strategies for cultivating gratitude and positivity.......................... 117

The importance of self-care in maintaining mental and emotional
well-being... 119

Conclusion 124

INTRODUCTION

Losing a spouse is one of life's most difficult and painful experiences. It can be hard to know where to begin the process of healing and rebuilding your life. Grief can be a long and complex journey, one that is different for everyone. This book is designed to be a guide for widows as they navigate the grieving process and work to find happiness again.

In this book, you will learn about the definition of grief and the stages of grief, and the importance of acknowledging and accepting it. The role of culture and societal expectations in grief will also be discussed, as well as the importance of self-care during this time.

You will also learn about the value of a strong support system during grief, and how to communicate your needs to loved ones. Alternative sources of support, such as therapy or support groups, will also be explored.

We will also delve into different coping mechanisms, such as therapy, support groups, and alternative ways like journaling and art therapy. Navigating practical tasks and responsibilities after the loss of a spouse will be discussed, as well as finding meaning and purpose after loss.

We will also cover common emotions experienced during grief, such as anger and guilt, and strategies for coping with and expressing difficult emotions. The process of rebuilding and creating a new normal and the role of goal-setting and planning for the future will also be discussed.

We hope this book will provide you with guidance, comfort, and hope as you navigate the grieving process and work to rebuild your life. It will also be an encouragement and support for readers as they navigate the grieving process and rebuild their lives.

CHAPTER 1:

INTRODUCTION TO GRIEF AND THE

GRIEVING PROCESS

This book is meant to guide you through the grieving stage of losing a husband, but you cannot be guided if you do not understand what you're going through. It is important you know exactly what grief is and how it manifests.

What is Grief

Grief is a natural reaction to loss or sorrow. It is described as "extreme grief" and includes a wide range of feelings of various intensities. The word itself is derived from the Latin verb gravare, which means to make heavy, through the Old French verb grever, which means to torment, load, or oppress. Grief today unquestionably seems thick, oppressive, and onerous.

Grieving hurts. It can be viewed as a form of love, albeit possibly the most agonizing. It is the conflict between loving someone or something and being unsure of how to act in their absence. It includes annoyance, rage, resentment, and even bitterness. Grief can, in fact, be a kind of love that doesn't give up. In his book A Grief Observed, renowned author C. S. Lewis succinctly expressed his sorrow over the loss of his wife:

"The act of life is different throughout. Her absence permeates everything like the sky.

When someone is grieving, there is no predetermined pattern that they must follow. Even though they are grieving the same loss, it is a profoundly unique experience, and no two people will have it the same way. Furthermore, just because you have gone through grief in the past does not guarantee that you will feel the same way when you go through it again. Grief is a universal emotion, despite how uniquely individualized it is. We all experience grief at various times in our life.

Causes of Grief

Most of us immediately respond when asked what causes grief by stating the loss of a loved one. And we would be right because this frequently elicits the strongest grieving reactions. However, as was mentioned earlier, there are numerous reasons for sorrow.

Indeed, a loss of any kind can cause grief:

• A failed relationship or a divorce.

• Loss of stability in one's finances or employment.

• Retirement.

• Decline in health.

• A loss of fertility or a miscarriage.

• The end of a friendship

• Loss of a household pet.

• The terrible sickness or prognosis of a loved one.

• A loss of safety after trauma.

• A family's home is lost.

• Giving up on a long-held goal, such as getting turned down for a job or a scholarship.

Although each of these losses (and more) might cause a loss reaction, not everyone will have the same experiences with each of these losses. The loss is always very personal, no matter what.

It is not inappropriate for you to grieve over something that another person might not. Whatever the reason for your sorrow, there is always help available.

The Grieving Process

As was mentioned, everyone has a unique experience of grieving. There is no predetermined process or right or wrong way to experience grief. The way someone grieves will vary depending on a variety of circumstances, including their personality, coping style, the gravity of the loss, and whether or not they practice any form of spirituality.

The grieving process can take a long time. It must be viewed as an unrestricted, ongoing process of healing. Others may find themselves grieving and processing their loss for years, while some people may start to get most of their sentiments and emotions over the loss under control in a few weeks or months. No matter what the person has gone through, it is crucial that they are treated with kindness and that they and those around them are patient.

How to deal with the grieving process

Grief is a necessary component of life. We may, however, develop a better understanding of grieving and work to accept and process our losses. Most people eventually manage to learn to live with or along with the loss and are able to lead fulfilled, generally happy lives, even though they may never truly "get over" a loss.

It's crucial to understand the many stages of the grieving process before you can start to process a loss. It's also critical to acknowledge

9

that your sentiments and emotions are both normal and unique to you. You might find it helpful to start by expressing your emotional discomfort and to attempt and embrace the fact that you will experience a wide range of varied and frequently unexpected emotions.

Even though it is always a very private event, it is crucial that you get assistance. Support is best provided by people who are familiar with you and are concerned about your mental and physical health.

When you are grieving, caring for your bodily needs is equally as crucial as caring for your mental needs. It's crucial to remember that while you may experience intense sadness and sorrow, grieving is not the same as depression.

What are the stages of grief?

If you have ever experienced loss and mourned (and most of us have, in some manner), you are aware that there are various stages that a person goes through when they experience loss.

Elisabeth Kübler-Ross, a Swiss Psychiatrist, created a model of the several stages of mourning for those facing their own mortality as a result of a terminal disease back in 1969. Later, regardless of the type of sorrow, the Kübler-Ross model was accepted as a tool to comprehend the mourning process generally.

Kübler-Ross' Five Stages of Grief were described as:

1. Denial.
2. Anger.
3. Bargaining.
4. Depression.
5. Acceptance.

Denial

"This isn't my life!"

Numbness and shock are frequent feelings following a loss. Accepting that the loss is irreparable is difficult. The denial stage of mourning frequently serves as a protective mechanism, enabling the person who has experienced a loss to take care of all that is required in the days that follow.

When someone passes away, this could include planning funeral services, for example. Confusion, worry, and shock over the loss are also typical feelings at this time, particularly if the loss was unexpected.

You can feel as though you are living someone else's life, or at the very least that someone else is watching your life from a distance. In order to allow us to go step-by-step while our minds adjust to reality, this stage of mourning slows down our processing.

Anger

"They should have done more! This isn't fair!"

Many people are unaware that fury is just as much a component of mourning as sadness is, that it is a very typical response to loss. When we feel out of control, our brain automatically switches to anger because it wants us to exert as much primitive control as possible. At this point, we can become aggressive.

The cause of the loss may be the focus of anger. Anger can be directed at the departed, at medical personnel for being unable to rescue the person, at ourselves for actions we took or actions we wish we had taken prior to the person's passing if it is a part of the grieving process for the loss of a spouse.

Feelings of rage are also frequently experienced, even when the loss is not a death. Such rage can be directed towards a group, an employer, or a person who inflicted the trauma or the loss

Our brains are designed to be defensive. They want us to look for answers to our issues, including how to deal with sadness. Even the most knowledgeable people occasionally find themselves pleading with God or their physicians to intervene and solve the issue, undo the damage, or return things to them as they were.

When a person realizes there is little, if anything, that can be done to change the situation, they may experience a sense of helplessness, which can also be associated with this phase.

Depression

"Life is worthless without them."

The loss feels more tangible and unavoidable as the emotional haze lifts and the terror and rage fade. At this point, our melancholy intensifies and depression settles in. We are beginning to understand that the loss is permanent and will not alter. People retreat and become more socially isolated as a result of the loss's greater severity.

People frequently associate depression as being the main aspect of grief. After a loss, feelings of sadness or protracted grief are extremely frequent. These emotions might be very strong and overpowering. Feelings of unreality, apathy, and restlessness are frequent at this time. Many people going through this period of grieving may try to find solace in substances like alcohol, drugs, or food, but doing so has its own set of issues.

For many people, depression does not always accompany a loss. This grieving stage may reappear months or years later. Dips back into despair are quite common, even for individuals who have passed the acceptance stage.

Acceptance

"It is hard, but I can be happy again."

After a loss, acceptance allows one to resume a fulfilling life in which plans for the future can be made. This is frequently thought of as "moving on" after a loss. The aim of the mourning process for a person who has experienced a loss is this stage. But it rarely happens right away, and sometimes getting there requires a lot of work.

Many people do not want to reach this point because they believe that if they do, they will have "lost" the value of the loss. However, it's critical that we acknowledge acceptance as a fact of life.

Even when we have reached acceptance, we must recognize that this does not mean that we have fully recovered from a loss or that it is no longer a substantial and occasionally crippling aspect of our lives. In fact, it is preferable to think of the stages of mourning as an interconnected process rather than a sequential one.

Many people who are mourning will discover that they dip in and out of the many phases of sorrow or become trapped in one. Those who have attained the acceptance stage of their loss may relapse at any point and at any time into the melancholy or even the angry stage.

As a result, it's critical to keep providing assistance to those who have experienced a loss, even years later.

Many people consider how they may assist others and make use of their negative experiences during the acceptance stage of mourning. People may participate in activities in their loved one's memory after they pass away, such as charity events or random acts of kindness.

Others share their stories with others in an effort to support individuals who are in the early stages of grieving by providing them with support from someone who has been in their position.

It is crucial to stress that everyone's experience of grieving will be unique, despite the fact that these five stages are universal. Even if the same person has a different loss or if two people experience the same loss, no two people's journeys through it will be the same. There are no good or bad emotions.

Marked Grief

When someone attempts to hide their sadness and does not deal with it or let it take its course, it is referred to as masked grief. Our bodies and minds are shrewd in that the initial shock and denial feelings are helpful to us in the immediate aftermath of a loss.

It implies that we are able to function even as we begin to process the loss. But if we let this stage of denial drag on for too long, we won't learn to accept the loss and move on.

We're used to hiding our feelings; many of us do it every day in a variety of settings to present a more conventional front. But covering up grief for a long time is unhealthy. After a loss, repressing your sentiments will cause them to surface in different ways.

Men or people from cultures and civilizations where there are "rules" about how one should behave after a loss are more likely to hide their sadness than women do. Masked grief can also be experienced by people who conceal their loss from others.

The Difference between grief and sadness

Even while sadness and grief frequently go hand in hand, they are distinct emotions. Sadness is a major component of grieving and frequently the main feeling that most of us experience after any form of loss. Sadness, however, does not adequately describe grief.

There are numerous other feelings that a person experiences during the mourning process in addition to those listed in the stages of grief, such as:

- Shock, disbelief, denial, and numbness.

- Guilt and regret.

- Panic, anxiety, and fear.

- Anger.

- Relief.

- Elation.

- Jealousy.

- Gratitude.

While grieving, any of these feelings are acceptable. There are other aspects of grief than sadness, which is a significant component.

Signs and symptoms of grief

The majority of us are aware of the emotional symptoms and indicators of sadness. However, grief's bodily effects are also very prevalent. If you are unsure of what is causing these symptoms, they may worry you.

The following are some physical indicators and symptoms of grief: •
Chest or throat tightness.

- An empty, hollow sensation in the stomach.
- Breathing problems.
- Weakness, tiredness, and fatigue.
- Noise sensitivity
- A parched mouth.
- A change in appetite.
- Pains and aches.
- Sleep issues and nightmares.

Many of the physical signs of mourning, particularly if the loss involved
a sick individual, might make the grieving person more anxious. It is
critical that the person seeks support because the symptoms, whether
brought on by grief or something else, are very much present.

Of course, we must also recognize the emotional indicators and effects
of mourning, to which we are frequently more accustomed. Grief's
emotional symptoms, such as sadness, despair, and rage, can become
so severe that they transform into a lengthy depressive episode that
requires medical care in the same way that a physical illness does.

Types of grief

The ordinary grieving process, also known as normal sorrow or
straightforward grief, is the one that most people use. Masked grief has
also been discussed previously. However, other types of sorrow are
more complicated and frequently call for additional care or therapy.

Complicated Grieving

This type of grief lasts far longer and is more incapacitating. For a
protracted time, it limits the person's capacity to lead a regular life.

Chronic Grieving: This occurs when the intense and overpowering feelings associated with grief continue to exist. In the stages of mourning known as bargaining and/or despair, the person frequently gets trapped.

Anticipatory Grief: This is the emotional response to a loss that was anticipated, like when a person passes away from a terminal illness. Therefore, the grieving process frequently starts before the actual loss. This is frequently unclear, and it does not imply that it will be simpler to deal with the loss of a spouse.

Secondary Loss

This occurs when the original loss causes a second loss. For instance, if your husband passes away, a secondary loss may include, among other things, losing your home or your income.

Cumulative Grief

This occurs when a person experiences multiple losses before processing the initial loss.

Absent Grief

This is when a person who has experienced a loss doesn't seem to be grieving and acts as if nothing has happened. When it persists for a long time, this is problematic.

Traumatic Grief

This is the sorrow that follows a loss that occurred under terrifying or violent conditions. An individual might get PTSD as a result of this.

Abbreviated Grief

This is a transient form of grief. When a person remarries soon after losing a spouse, it is frequently considered that their grieving is "gone" rather than actually having occurred.

Ambiguous Grief or a Disenfranchised Loss

This occurs when someone loses something that is unclear to them or to others. As an illustration, it might be the sorrow that an infertile person feels. This type of grieving may not be recognized by others, and it is frequently not supported, which can have long-lasting implications.

Is grief a mental health problem?

Grief can undoubtedly result in mental health issues, but these issues are often not diagnosable. Grief strains our life and takes a long time to process. The grief-related feelings and emotions persist even after we have accepted a loss. A person typically gains the ability to control these emotions over time.

When the symptoms of grieving do not go away in a conventional fashion, as they do in complicated grief, it becomes a mental health issue. In this situation, it is more difficult than easier to control the symptoms of mourning, and they have a protracted negative impact on a person's everyday activities.

Whether or not a person's grieving is or develops into a mental health issue, it is crucial that there is assistance during and after the process.

The importance of acknowledging and accepting grief

Grief is a normal aspect of how we deal with upsetting and painful experiences. In my integrative medicine clinic, many of the patients must learn how to talk about their sadness or other emotions for the first time. Unfortunately, it seems that we have learned to hide or avoid dealing with our emotions in our fast-paced world because we believe we don't have enough time.

Long-term feeling suppression has the drawback that our bodies eventually yearn to deal with and express those feelings. Your body may compel you to deal with your sentiments later on, whether you want to or not if you don't let it attend to them through its natural healing process. Other symptoms of sadness or mourning include discomfort, exhaustion, insomnia, or a worsening of pre-existing medical conditions.

So let's spend some time figuring out the best ways to handle sadness and loss before we shift to talking about our sentiments about the numerous recent natural catastrophes, the magnificent heroes who have died attempting to save us, and those who are still playing that selfless role today. Unfortunately, given the number of terrible occurrences that occur, I would not advise any of my patients—or, by extension, my readers—to conceal their emotions over an extended period of time. However, there are occasions when it may be okay to put grief on hold until we can handle it more skillfully. This gets us to the topic of the first stage of mourning, which includes denial, shock, and numbness. It appears that many of us act in this way.

Although I included the list of possible grief stages, I wish to admonish readers that they might not apply to everyone. We all have various coping mechanisms for grief because we are all unique. You can better comprehend what might happen when something horrific happens and we have to deal with it by understanding the phases of grieving.

Potentially, you may experience numbness, shock, or denial during the initial stages of bereavement. In order to be able to escape danger or give ourselves the time to deal with the practical aspects of the loss or terrible incident, this phase helps to shield us from the initial effect of the event. This is a defense mechanism to prevent us from being overtaken by distressing experiences and to give us some time to escape if necessary. In addition, it provides us time to process the information gradually rather than all at once when the event initially occurs, allowing us to fully appreciate its significance.

The negotiation phase is normally the next stage. As we act out the incident, we begin to consider what we may have done differently and whether we might have changed the outcome in any way. It's crucial that we get through this stage successfully so that we can heal and avoid becoming mired in feelings of severe guilt or unresolved issues.

The next stage is when we experience melancholy, loneliness, and depression. It is crucial that you ask for assistance if you need it throughout this stage. In this stage of mourning, support from loved ones, therapists, or support groups can be extremely beneficial. I would strongly advise involving your doctor in this stage of the recovery process. Your doctor can assist you in recognizing the warning signs and determine whether any supplements or drugs are necessary if you are feeling more depressed than is simply normal during a time of loss or grief.

You could experience feelings of indignation and unfairness as you move past the pain of the loss. The phase of fury is a normal stage of recovery from sadness. The involvement of your doctor and loved ones, as well as support and counseling, are crucial throughout this stage. If you aren't used to these emotions and haven't figured out how to effectively handle them, this stage could be very daunting.

You learn to accept the loss and incorporate it into your life during the acceptance phase. It's less important that you're ok with the tragedy or loss. Instead, you are able to incorporate the occurrences into your regular thoughts and feelings when your mind, body, and emotions are finally able to accept what has happened.

Many of my patients believe that experiencing grief for an extended period of time is abnormal. They frequently ponder things like, "Shouldn't I be over it by now? " or "Shouldn't I still be angry about this?" It's crucial to realize that healing can take an as long or as little time as your body requires to recover from severe losses and catastrophes. We are all unique, and none of my patients are identical cookie-cutter copies of one another, as I always remind them. The widely accepted theory of the phases of grief might give you a general idea of how one individual can approach grieving, but in the end, everyone's grieving experience is unique to some degree.

Be kind to yourself and give yourself as much or as little time as you require to heal, as long as you are receiving the support and assistance you require during this time (and a competent healthcare practitioner is keeping an eye out for any alarming symptoms or feelings). It's acceptable and natural to go back to a previous stage of the grieving process whenever you choose.

In the end, each person's experience of sorrow is somewhat unique, and each person may have a distinct experience during each episode. We utilize the phases of grieving as a general framework to understand why we experience certain emotions at different stages of healing. However, just because your grief is a little different does not imply that you are not "normal." This is the same reason I typically advise my patients to find support groups or therapists, and I advise my readers to ask their doctors for advice on how to cope with a challenging healing process.

Without a doubt, the constant calamities and senseless tragedies we witness on television these days have increased our awareness of loss and grief. At my own clinic, I observed this repeatedly.

We can use this moment to teach ourselves and those around us how to properly manage our emotions rather than stifle them, even though we cannot stop natural disasters or senseless tragedies (no matter how much we wish we could).

If we are able to accept the negatives, feel their influence, and become stronger from them by allowing ourselves to cope with all the emotions that go along with these events, we can be stronger and better equipped to bear the strains of life as a whole.

The role of culture and societal expectations in grief

When talking about the grieving process, it's necessary to take cultural and societal expectations into account. How people react to loss can be profoundly influenced by the beliefs and expectations that different cultures have around death and mourning. In Western nations, social expectations and standards frequently influence how people grieve and how long the process takes. Additionally, as there are frequently differing expectations for men and women in terms of how they should process their feelings, gender disparities can also affect how people react to sorrow.

Society's expectations, in addition to cultural norms, can influence how people grieve. These expectations can relate to topics such as how long it is acceptable to mourn, how to do so in a way that is acceptable to others, and how to move on following a loss. Depending on the culture, some may place a greater focus on honoring the deceased and observing a lengthier period of grieving. Other cultures could have different expectations, such as a speedier timetable for moving on and a more stoic approach to grieving.

Understanding how culture and societal norms play a part in how people feel sorrow might assist. When discussing the grieving process, it's crucial to take into account the values, standards, and customs of each person's culture.

CHAPTER 2:

EFFECTS OF GRIEF

Grief can affect your physical and emotional state in many several ways. Even as a woman, these effects can severely upset you and how you function.

Physical

Your body may enter a serious condition of stress as a result of your emotional reaction to losing your husband. The body goes into shock as a result of an increase in stress hormones being released into the bloodstream.

The body's reaction to these stress hormones determines the severity and length of the symptoms. Acute stress manifests physically in symptoms such as:

- Loss of energy and fatigue.
- Pains in the body and head.
- Stomach pain, nausea, vomiting, weight loss or increase, under- or overeating insomnia, and excessive slumber.
- Chest discomfort and breathlessness.
- Dehydration and dry mouth.
- The immune system is weakened.
- Memory loss and mental fuzz.

Grief may also be accompanied by additional reactions to acute stress and a compromised immune system, including but not restricted to: Hair loss

- An enlarged tongue.
- Fainting.
- Blood pressure problems.
- Low blood sugar levels
- Bronchitis.
- Clots of blood.
- Heartburn.

This extensive list of bodily signs demonstrates that grieving is a serious issue. Our bodies are working overtime to try and achieve the same thing as our minds work to intellectually digest the feelings of losing a loved one.

Let's explore what is happening with the main grieving symptoms.

Fatigue & energy loss.

All of our internal resources are working overtime to repair and return everything to normal as our body releases stress hormones. When a loved one passes away, this might cause us to feel heavy and worn out.

I spent roughly six months curled up in a fetal position after being highly active.

Your body needs to rest when you're grieving. As your body is telling you to take it easy at this time, give yourself permission to rest. Your life just lost a significant portion, therefore it will take some time for your energy levels to return to normal.

Take a nap if your body is requesting one, and remember to be patient and gentle with yourself.

Headaches & body pains.

Our bodies can become incredibly uncomfortable as a result of the stress brought on by sadness. Common after-loss symptoms include headaches, migraines, generalized muscular discomfort, and heaviness that can even resemble the illness. In elderly persons, grief can exacerbate health conditions already present.

And regrettably, crying, a typical response to death can make these pains worse.

Ibuprofen, cold compresses, and other remedies can ease this pain temporarily, but you should be careful not to use numbing as a coping mechanism to avoid experiencing the grieving symptoms (more on this later).

Nausea, vomiting, stomach pain, digestive issues, weight loss/gain & under/overeating.

We store a lot of tension in our stomachs, which can cause problems with eating and digestion. The symptoms of our body's stress response include nausea, stomach pain, diarrhea, and the sensation that your stomach is in knots.

- "Unfortunately, I've reverted to my previous behavior and have relapsed with my eating issue. Since my father's murder on August 29th, I've dropped almost 40 pounds.
- "I just don't feel hungry at all right now."

- "On my first try, I felt bad for eating something while he couldn't. Even though I am aware that it is not good thinking, it is what it is.
- "Eating is very difficult for me. I have no desire to eat.

Even if you're not hungry, it's crucial to receive the nutrition your body needs during this time. To give your body the energy it needs to get back on track, try to eat three meals a day. Avoid foods that are hot, acidic, or foreign because they will strain your digestive system more.

Some people have the propensity to use food as a coping mechanism for dealing with difficult emotions. Therefore, some people may also experience problems with consuming and losing weight.

Call a friend or see your doctor for support if your physical reaction to grief prevents you from maintaining a healthy, balanced diet. You don't have to do this alone, and your body really does need you right now.

Insomnia & oversleeping.

Grief can keep us up all night with accompanying emotional turmoil and lingering thoughts. On the other hand, the exhaustion brought on by emotional stress can also cause us to oversleep, wake up feeling groggy, and need more sleep.

To assist your circadian rhythm so that you sleep more regularly, do everything in your power to be outside throughout the day so that you can be exposed to Vitamin D.

And if your racing thoughts are keeping you up at night, consider listening to a guided meditation for sleep to help you unwind and fall asleep easily.

Shortness of breath & chest pain.

Extreme stress, such as that brought on by the loss of a spouse, is linked to alterations in coronary blood arteries or heart muscle cells (or both), which prevent the left ventricle from contracting properly. This disease is known as stress-induced cardiomyopathy as well as a broken-heart syndrome. Chest pain and shortness of breath are symptoms that are similar to a heart attack.

Broken hearts are genuine and should be taken seriously.

- "Two weeks after my mother passed away this year, my heart started racing, and I had to have heart surgery. If you have ongoing medical issues, visit the doctor frequently, or wear a heart monitor, you might require additional surgery.
- "About two months after he died away, I experienced a small heart attack. One physician referred to it as "broken heart syndrome."

Do not hesitate to seek medical assistance from your primary care physician if you are experiencing breathing difficulties or chest discomfort. Start by letting them know that you are grieving the loss of your husband and want to ensure that your heart health is unharmed.

Dry mouth & dehydration.

It's normal to suffer dry mouth and dehydration at this time because of the time you've spent sobbing and everything else going on in your body.

To keep everything in balance during this period, your body needs more liquids. Always keep a bottle of water on you and sip on it even when you're not thirsty. Try your best to avoid drinking too much soda or coffee.

Use the color of your urine as a surrogate for your hydration levels if you're unsure if you're well hydrated. Better, the more precise.

Weakened immune system.

It's only a matter of time before something breaks if you drive a car at full power for a long time. Your body, which is going through the grieving process, is experiencing the same thing.

You are more prone to illness and other health problems because your body is producing stress hormones on overdrive. In the background, immune cell function deteriorates and inflammatory responses increase in bereaved individuals.

"I've experienced bronchitis on several occasions."

Keep this in mind as you navigate your grief. Try your best to maintain a clean face and hands, stay away from sick people, and engage in healthy exercise, eating, sleeping, and leisure activities.

Brain fog & forgetfulness.

When someone close to you passes away, it might feel like the world is being shattered, causing bewilderment, forgetfulness, and difficulty focusing.

It's usual to become absorbed in one's thoughts and fervent longing for a loved one.

Use to-do lists, schedules, calendar reminders, and phone notifications to help you stay on task if you're feeling disoriented and forgetful. The fog should clear out with time.

Mental Health Conditions Caused By Grief

Grief is frequently accompanied by mental health disorders, which, if addressed, can also develop into further physical symptoms. among the ailments are:

- Depression (insomnia, suicidal thoughts, loss of appetite, mental and physical sluggishness, persistent feelings of worthlessness, extreme hopelessness).
- Panic and anxiety attacks.
- Nightmares and night terrors.
- Self-flagellation (picking fingernails).

Everybody's body and brain react differently to sorrow, and some people may benefit from medication in the short term to balance the hormone imbalance while long-term strategies like therapy and holistic treatments are used concurrently.

It's crucial to visit a doctor if you have any of these symptoms or if your mourning symptoms get worse. By doing this, you can seek your doctor's expert advice and start back on the path to a good recovery.

Ways to Cope With the Physical Effects of Grief

There is no single treatment for grieving, as seen by the extensive range of bodily signs of grief.

There are bandages we can apply to the pain to try and make it go away, but real healing happens when we face the anguish, sit with it, and figure out a new way to live.

Practice mindfulness.

The practice of mindfulness-based stress reduction is an excellent method to face your discomfort and become conscious of how it affects your body and thinking.

You can start by enrolling in an online course that teaches you the benefits of mindfulness, and how it works and provides you with the tools you need to practice at home.

Then, you can repeatedly return to your breath and the present moment by using mindfulness techniques. a capability that will enable you to start controlling your feelings and the stress hormones that lead to the physical symptoms of mourning.

Get the right amount of rest.

Try to get 8 hours of sleep each night at the same time. Allow yourself to relax if you need to sleep during the day.

Try the following to promote restful sleep:

- For assistance in settling into a relaxed state, try guided meditations.
- Spend 15 minutes each morning outside in the sun.
- Before going to bed, apply lavender oil to your pillow.
- When the sun goes down, avoid using electronics with blue light.

Eat the right amount of nutritious food.

Eat three balanced meals every day that is high in protein, fiber, and healthy fats. Make sure to eat vegetables at least once a day, preferably with each meal.

Take a workout.

Do something to move your body every day, even if it's just a 5-minute walk outside. Increase the length of your stroll or add more exercise over time to make your body perspire.

Head outdoors (preferably in nature).

You may completely rejuvenate your mind, body, and soul in nature. Get outside and practice being conscious of the smells, sounds, sights, and textures around you, even if you only lay in the grass at a nearby park or in a hammock in your backyard.

Consider socializing.

The joyful hormones you get from being among other people will benefit you in the long run, even if it will feel strange to return to normal life with a broken heart and physical signs of sadness.

Ask a friend or member of your family to join you for a low-key first activity by calling them. Maybe invite them over for tea at your house or ask them to meet you for a walk in the park.

Try new (or old) hobbies.

You may start living your life again by taking time to relax and have fun. Is there anything you can do to celebrate the life of your loved one?

Try adding something to your schedule when you're ready, then keep to it. Showing up will probably be the most difficult aspect.

Be a part of a grieving support group.

During this trying time in your life, finding a grief counselor or a support group might make you feel less alone. Find local support groups in your area by searching online.

Steer clear of poor coping strategies.

It will be simple to use alcohol, cigarettes, and other unhealthy coping techniques to dull the pain of loss, but abstaining from them will be essential for your long-term healing.

You don't have to do it alone; remember that facing your suffering will aid your long-term healing. A qualified grief counselor or therapist can assist you in navigating the complexity of your feelings and physical symptoms.

Emotional Effects

You're prone to experience conflicting emotions, which can frequently leave you perplexed. You must constantly remind yourself that these are typical responses to a loss and that they pass.

Other symptoms, such as the inability to accept what has happened and acts of denial, are coping methods. They help you deal with the things you need to do, such as registering the death, locating a funeral director, dealing with utility providers and banks, etc., by easing some of the stress and trauma associated with your loss.

You might be inclined to put on a brave front and suffer in silence in these circumstances, but holding it in will probably lead to problems down the road. It's crucial to deal with your emotions and ask for assistance when you need it.

Some of the most typical emotional consequences of grieving and losing a spouse include the following:

Initial shock

Even when it was anticipated, a loved one's passing nevertheless shocks us. Disbelief and a minor loss of connection to reality frequently follow. Like most other mourning symptoms, the first shock eventually fades away, but if it lingers, you should speak with a skilled support person.

Panic and Anxiety

Various feelings and emotions that are triggered by your loss might be rather strong and overpowering, especially in the beginning. It's likely to cause you to reflect on both your own and other people's mortality. Additionally, it may cause you to feel uncomfortable and provoke some of your phobias. You must schedule a consultation with your GP if these feelings don't get better over time.

Anger

Anger can rise up as you realize the significance of your loss. You can observe that you lose your temper easily and become upset at people or at yourself for your loss. You might even harbor resentment toward the deceased.

Anger is a common and fleeting response to your loss, despite the fact that it can lead to conflict and upset the harmony of your relationships with family members or friends. You should get assistance if it doesn't go better on its own over time or if you feel like you're endangering both yourself and other people.

Guilt

It's common to feel guilty after your husband passes away. It can be because you are the one still alive and not your loved one, or it might be because you feel like you didn't do enough to stop their death. Although guilt feelings are personal and situational, just like the other mourning effects and symptoms, they are a typical response to loss.

It is beneficial to reflect on the kind things you have done for the departed or to ask family and friends for comfort and support.

Sadness

Sadness and sorrow go hand in hand, and they are two of the most typical emotional reactions to the loss of a spouse. You are likely to experience them as soon as you start to notice your loss and its effects, even though they don't usually become obvious right immediately. At that point, you start to consider the person who has passed away and how much you still miss them. At this point, these emotions and thoughts are perfectly normal.

You should make an effort to fight the impulse to isolate yourself and stay in touch with other people. Talking to trusted individuals about your loss and feelings might be beneficial.

You can join a local or online grieving support group if you don't feel comfortable doing this.

Staying Strong

Please remember to set aside time to deal with your mourning if your circumstances call for you to put your grief to one side and be strong for other family members.

Speaking with your parents, kids, or other family members who might depend on you or need your support might be advantageous to them as well. These discussions also aid in dispelling any misconceptions and presumptions you or they may have had. Consider joining a support group or seeking out a grief counselor if you're not prepared for that.

The importance of allowing oneself to feel and express emotions

The old adages of "stiff upper lip" and "keep calm and carry on" are woven deeply inside our collective subconscious.

So it makes sense that when someone has a very catastrophic loss that triggers strong emotions, their initial response is frequently to turn away from the intensity, repress the feelings, and attempt to move on with their lives. And in many respects, this is adaptive because it enables us to keep our stability, our careers, and our relationships even while we deal with a serious loss. But like with everything in life, moderation is the key, therefore we must be sure to give our emotions the time and space they require while simultaneously attempting to preserve stability.

Consequently, let's address the subject of "Why is expressing emotion vital for those who are grieving?"

Emotions are designed to move

The Latin root of the word "emotion" means "to move."

"Emotion is a brain impulse that propels an organism to action," claims Science Daily.

The word emotion has been linked to motion since its inception. Consider the phrases we use to express emotional events, like "that truly moved me" or "I was stirred up."

We process emotion mostly through movement. With this in mind, it is clear why emotion cannot simply be ignored, repressed, or avoided. Thoughts like "just get on with things" or "stop thinking about it and you'll feel better" can sound like good strategies when people are dealing with the intense emotion that comes with grief because they feel afraid and ill-equipped to handle the pain and distress. As a result, outdated cultural narratives take over and make these ideas sound like good advice.

Ways to express yourself

How can I shift the emotions so they don't become stuck? maybe on your mind. Herein lies the importance of emotional expression. The good news is that getting those feelings moving can usually be done in a very natural and easy way! I'm referring to basic emotional expression techniques that most individuals are naturally aware of.

It's usually sufficient to cry when you're unhappy, stamp your feet when you're angry, or chat with a supportive friend when you're feeling overwhelmed.

Express your sentiments in a concrete way

There are a number of original, easy ways to express emotion that you might not instantly consider (and sometimes even comforting or fun).

Maintain a healthy body

Your mind and body are intertwined, and emotional and physical recovery go hand in hand. It's normal to feel tired or low energy, but if you can go for a run or stroll, it will speed up the process. Get the right amount of sleep to combat your exhaustion, and eat meals that will provide you energy as well as comfort.

Allow yourself to grieve

Often, we numb our pain by occupying ourselves with duties or hobbies. Avoiding grief simply makes it last longer; it must be allowed to come to the surface. Depression, anxiety, substance misuse, and other health issues can result from unresolved bereavement.

Never let anyone or yourself judge you

You are free to mourn for whatever long and how deeply you need to. Nobody can tell you when to "move on" or "get over it," not even yourself. You should allow for moments of delight in your mourning and don't feel guilty about them if you experience anger, crying, not crying, or even laughing.

Chapter 3:

Finding support from friends and family

Grief is a complex feeling that is full of paradoxes.

Even while it seems to us like time is moving slowly, it actually isn't. We try to avoid thinking about death even though we can't stop thinking about it. We are both strong and weak. We are vulnerable even while we are resilient.

Our task of mourning includes accepting and appreciating these important paradoxes, as well as others. Balance and back-and-forth are key here. While there isn't a universal formula that works for everyone, you'll discover that working each day to find the balance that works for you can help you move forward.

The need for isolation versus social support is another conflict in grieving that is crucial for you to investigate. What is superior? The reply is "both"

The Need For Solitude In Grief

Many of us are accustomed to grieving alone. We frequently retreat inside when we are torn apart emotionally and spiritually. Early grief creeps up on you like a fog. We may frequently find ourselves afterward entangled in our own inner sensations and thoughts. That is typical.

The useful inner experience of being bogged down in your grief is frequently referred to as "sitting in your wound." You give in to grief when you allow yourself to sit in the wound. You give in to the want to slow down and inwardly turn. You give yourself permission to properly wallow in your suffering. For a while, you close the door on the outside world in order to finally make room to let it back in.

When we are grieving, we require quiet, alone time to process our emotions and ideas. Sometimes we need to intentionally pursue solitude in order to slow down and turn inside. It's not a curse to be alone, despite what we may have been thinking. Actually, it is a blessing. We are alone when we are born and alone when we pass away. Each of us is a special individual and a child of the universe.

Grieving alone is both important and therapeutic. However, if you constantly divert yourself, keep busy, or become attached to others in order to avoid being alone, you can be putting off your natural, essential discomfort. You might be blocking out the quiet, inner voice that is telling you to slow down, look inward, and pay attention to it. You can be ignoring your soul and spirit. Your grieving process will then stall. You become mired in denial and avoidance.

Be aware that both too little and too much solitude can be detrimental during a time of bereavement. The griever who entirely closes off from the outside world and refuses to accept and acknowledge the support of others can likewise become stuck.

The Need For Social Support In Grief

To receive and accept assistance from friends, family, neighbors, and coworkers is one of our fundamental needs during a time of grieving. We may convey our natural and necessary pain to others thanks to their empathy. Every time we discuss our sorrow and relate our love-and-loss experiences, we are moving closer to healing.

Humans require company, therefore social support during a difficult time is essential. We are social beings, and our connections give life significance. In fact, our own grief bears witness to this reality. Our lives had purpose because of the connection we shared with the deceased. Other partnerships in our ongoing life are the same way.

We feel lonely when we have no friends. After the loss of a special person, especially one who had been a part of our everyday life, loneliness can be difficult. Being alone hurts. We need to discover ways to connect with others in order to combat our loneliness.

We have the ability to create new habits for spending time with friends, family, neighbors, coworkers, fellow volunteers, individuals from our local community, people who share our interests, and other people. Working on connection not only makes us feel less alone but also gives us listening ears for when we need to share our sorrow.

During our times of mourning, the social assistance we want and receive aids in creating a meaningful bridge that leads us into the future. Death may have put an end to a cherished relationship, but we can still build and enhance new connections. Even while they can never fully replace the deceased, these people can and will restore meaning to our existence.

Being an introvert might make asking for and accepting social support difficult. But I guarantee that developing a closer bond with even one other person will improve your life in a variety of ways and support you during this difficult period. No man is an island, as the poet John Donne memorably penned. In times of sadness, this is never more true.

Finding A Balance

I sincerely hope you would make an effort to strike the correct mix between solitude and social support while you are grieving. Momentum is one sign to look for. Do you feel as though you are moving along in your journey? (Backward movement occasionally is OK.) Do you sense the optimism that comes with action?

On the other side, if you are feeling helpless or stuck, you may need to deliberately work on your solitude / social support balance. Try setting out some time for actual solitude or sincere social engagement if you tend to err on one side or the other, or if you don't genuinely engage in either but instead spend your time on meaningless distractions (or both). Both your present and your future will change as a result.

How to communicate your needs to loved ones

When a family member or loved one passes away, those who care about you make an effort to support you however they can. Others may bring you food. Some ask you to participate in organized activities or to spend time in a relaxed environment. Some people believe that keeping your mind busy with a job and hobbies is preferable. Others anticipate that when you are grieving, you won't participate in work or other activities. When it comes to coping with sorrow, everyone has various needs and expectations. In order for your friends and family to support you when you're mourning, you must let them know what you need from them.

Everyone Approaches Grieving Differently

Everyone has a different concept of what grieving looks like—your friends, family, and coworkers included. Their attitudes toward you during a time of grief are influenced by their beliefs and expectations.

It's your responsibility to express your needs. Let them know when their well-intended suggestions fit with your grief process and when they don't.

Communicate Your Needs Clearly and Without Guilt

When you are mourning, the people who care about you will want to do and say completely well-intentioned things. Individuals who are mourning find it challenging to express their needs without feeling guilty as a result. It could be challenging to tell a family member to stop baking casseroles for you when you just want it to stop, especially if you know she is only trying to help.

Recognize that you are the one going through this sadness; you shouldn't feel bad for expressing your needs. Just be straightforward about it. Show gratitude for the kind things that others do. Demand actions that aren't being taken. Tell others what isn't working. You should start your sentence with something like:

- "I appreciate your efforts to help. Instead, it would be helpful if...
- "I value your perspectives on loss. I need you to respect that my experience is different from yours.
- "I appreciate everything you've been doing. What I really require is

Just say it. Telling someone you don't want them to do anything is acceptable. Additionally, it's acceptable to request something that your friends or family aren't doing.

Needs Change

Your needs will alter as the grief process progresses. Whatever mourning theories you hold dear, grief following the loss of a family member or loved one is believed to go through a number of stages, according to specialists. As you progress through this process, you may need to convey your needs several times because each of these phases will require various things from you. Feel free to request the exact opposite of what you required the previous week. Your loved ones are aware that your needs and emotions will alter over time.

The most important thing to keep in mind while articulating your wants is to actually do it. Inform your loved ones about your needs. Don't allow someone to continue acting in a way that depresses, infuriates, irritates, or upsets you. They're attempting to assist, so let them know what you need by expressing your needs.

Exploring alternative sources of support, such as therapy or support groups

Following the death of a spouse, people are frequently advised to "check out a bereavement support group." And it's not a terrible idea either. Participation in grief and loss support groups has several advantages.

What is Bereavement?

Attending a grieving support group is typically the first option that comes to mind when looking for a support group for the loss of a spouse, but there are other bereavement support groups. You are guided through the grieving process via bereavement support. Both grief and grieving take place during this period as people adjust to their losses. If you're wondering whether a bereavement support group rather than a grief support group will help, the answer is yes. It might make it simpler for you to deal with your loss in a different way.

The advantages of joining a support group

Numerous configurations and sizes are available for grief support groups. Sometimes they are unique to a certain kind of disaster or loss. They may also be less specific. A licensed therapist, counselor, or religious leader may occasionally serve as the session's facilitator. The group occasionally is led by a certified volunteer. Regardless, the shared experience of losing a spouse is what unites the group. A grief support group has the following five advantages:

1. Offers Hope

The journey of grief has turns and straightaways, stops, and beginnings. Even while every experience is unique, everyone who experiences loss does so. People who are just beginning their trip can connect with those who are much further along by congregating in a group. Meeting and conversing with people who have suffered a comparable loss demonstrates the possibility of regaining joy. Sharing such comfort can give those who are farther along in their healing process crucial self-validation and confirmation that the group is a valuable resource for others.

2. You're not by yourself.

The reassurance that you are not alone is perhaps the largest advantage of a grief support group. When everyone around you seems to be "moving on with their lives," grieving may be incredibly lonely and isolated. You might discover that other individuals share your experiences, sentiments, and challenges by joining a support group for parent loss. We've been there, the support group community says when your loss becomes overpowering. We comprehend you. This is a strong message made at a crucial moment.

3. A Different Viewpoint

No two grief journeys are the same, as we noted earlier, and must stress again. However, others who have suffered a comparable loss can be able to offer insightful counsel, helpful recommendations, or a different point of view. You might get some practical insights through listening and learning that will aid you as you continue on your grieving journey.

4. Providing Support

People gain a sense of purpose and meaning by giving to others. This generosity might be a beneficial tool for the recovery process. When you take part in a support group for people who have lost a spouse, you not only get guidance but also have the opportunity to share your story and motivate others. When we help someone on their path, we become aware of how far along we have come on our own journey.

5. The Feeling of Belonging

Humans have a natural desire to fit in and be a part of a tribe or community. For thousands of years, this drive for survival has been quite helpful to mankind. Indeed, research suggests that a sense of community can enhance our general pleasure. After a loss, you could feel isolated or excluded and different from other people due to your sadness. Finding a community that accepts and understands you might be a crucial step in your healing. Nobody wants to join the grieving club, but if you do, you could find comfort in the company of fellow members.

Chapter 4:

Exploring Different Coping

Mechanisms

The role of therapy in grief recovery

Everyone grieves differently, and it can be experienced in many different ways, including emotionally, physically, and spiritually.

During the grieving process, shock, anger, grief, guilt, and worry are frequent and overwhelming emotions. There may occasionally be no feelings, just numbness. Some people find it hard to move on from their loss and think they'll never experience happiness again.

Grief counseling provides assistance during this trying time. It is a type of therapy that aids grieving in exploring and sorting through upsetting and perplexing emotions.

After a loss, it's normal to feel alone and lonely, which is why having family and friends by your side can be so helpful. Even though they are also suffering, it isn't always feasible to express your grief openly and freely among them. While some families and cultures believe that grieving must be suffered stoically and promptly resolved, others encourage support groups that last only until the funeral, after which everyone is left to make their own decisions.

Counseling sessions give those who are grieving alone a place to vent all of their feelings while also validating their sentiments. If a group of family members or couples wants to discover more efficient ways to assist one another, they can go to counseling sessions together.

There are five phases of mourning, according to the Kübler-Ross theory: denial, anger, bargaining, depression, and acceptance. However, there is frequently no clear path from the agony of loss to relief. Some people never move past a certain stage, while others advance only to repeatedly regress to prior phases. Grief can sometimes be put off, only to reappear weeks or months later.

Grief counseling helps people as they grieve in their own style and at their own pace rather than trying to hasten the process.

A grief counselor discusses the mourning process and assists the person in creating a new, fruitful relationship with their deceased loved one. Counseling helps the bereaved get to a place where they can cope, make decisions, and move on.

When grief overwhelms

Prolonged grief disorder may be present when grief lasts a long time and interferes with daily life. The following signs and symptoms are associated with chronic sorrow, according to the American Psychological Association:

- A deep-seated longing for the deceased.
- Having a hard time accepting death.
- severe emotional suffering.
- emotional detachment.
- The sensation of losing a piece of oneself.
- ongoing depression.
- Absence from customary social activities.

Generally speaking, the loss of a partner is common in this form of grieving. Additionally, a quick or violent death may have caused it.

A 2017 meta-analysis found that up to 10% of persons who have lost a loved one may experience protracted bereavement disorder.

Obtaining grief counseling

Counseling for bereavement is offered by the majority of therapists. If counseling is out of your financial range, many mental health professionals provide a sliding scale. Consider participating in regional and online support networks. Request a mental health specialist's referral from your physician. You can find a counselor nearby or online by visiting the following websites:

- American Psychiatric Association
- Anxiety & Depression Association of America
- Black Mental Health Alliance
- Mental Health America
- What's Your Grief?
- World Professional Association for Transgender Health's (WPATH)

How therapy for grief can help

After a loss, seeking counseling can help you get over anxiety and despair by allowing you to absorb the event at your own pace.

Cognitive behavioral therapy (CBT) and acceptance and commitment therapy (ACT) are two techniques frequently used for bereavement. Each mental health professional may use a different approach to help people deal with sorrow.

1. Cognitive behavioral therapy

For mental health problems such as depression, anxiety, and post-traumatic stress disorder, CBT is a frequent treatment strategy (PTSD).

The therapist will assist you in recognizing harmful thought patterns that may influence your behaviors throughout a CBT session.

To address how these thoughts affect your mood and behavior, they can ask you to examine thoughts about loss and mourning as well as other unproductive ones. They can assist you in reducing the impact by using techniques like behavior targeting, reinterpreting, and reframing.

2. Acceptance and commitment therapy

Another approach to coping with loss and grief is ACT.

A 2016 study funded by the American Counseling Association found that by urging clients to practice mindfulness in order to accept their experience, ACT may also be beneficial for those experiencing protracted, difficult grieving.

For bereavement counseling, ACT employs the following six key processes:

1. Accepting unpleasant feelings. This phase entails being open to confronting and accepting unfavorable feelings and thoughts.
2. Cognitive Defusion. In order to study and understand emotions, this procedure includes separating from them.
3. Making contact with the present. ACT urges people to concentrate on the present because that is when change is possible and when you actually experience life.

4. Self as the setting. This level entails watching oneself go through your experiences or being an observer of your own life's experiences.

5. Values. These are the beliefs you have, and they guide how you live.

6. Determined action. This stage, which is the completion of the ACT, entails acting and overcoming challenges through navigating the earlier processes.

Types of therapy and how to find a therapist

You might require further support if you are struggling to deal with your loss and sadness. The finest suggestion is to talk to and confide in someone who understands and empathizes. A person who can truly assist you.

It could be a friend, neighbor, relative, medical professional, clergyman, or bereavement counselor. If you are fortunate enough to have a compassionate friend or relative, you may not need professional grief therapy.

1. Be Careful of Spending Too Much Time on Grief Forums.

These days, there are several bereavement forums, including specialized ones for various sorts of loss. Again, take caution as these can be quite valuable. Don't read about other people's tragedies for hours on end. You could find it to be excessively tiring and sad. Move on after finding solace in the fact that you are not alone in your sorrow.

2. Grief Counseling and Grief Therapy

Most medical facilities, doctors, funeral homes, and hospitals can connect you with a nearby grief counseling program. Alternatively, search the Internet or your local directory.

Today, there are also great, convenient, and completely private online grief therapy options. We suggest BetterHelp.com for their knowledgeable advice.

If it doesn't initially work, don't be upset. It's possible that you weren't meant to be with this person. If, after a few sessions, you are still not feeling better, don't be afraid to change therapists and find someone else.

Grief Support Groups - Pros and Cons

Group meetings might be beneficial occasionally. If you don't find them useful, do move on. Some are top-notch, while others might not be for you. Group dynamics are important. Some are successful while others are not.

It can be upsetting and challenging to listen to other really sad people. Even counselors occasionally need to decompress because they experience so much suffering. It may be more difficult if you are weak.

Attending these groups carries the risk that it will turn into a contest about who is suffering the most. "At least you got to say goodbye," "at least you didn't have to see her suffer".

Be cautious while engaging with these organizations, even though it may be comforting to feel less alone. Move on if you feel that it is aggravating the situation and that you are absorbing too much of others' sorrow. Find a strong, upbeat companion that you can chat with and who can join you in more enjoyable activities.

Alternative coping mechanisms, such as journaling or art therapy

Perhaps you're not quite ready for a one-on-one with a therapist or meetings with a support group, there are a number of great alternatives you could practice instead

1. Expressing your emotions

Talking to people about how you are feeling can help you cope with loss. Inform your friends that you merely want to express your feelings or think back on the person you've lost and don't need their advice or replies.

2. Keeping a journal

Putting your thoughts and feelings down on paper not only aids in the processing of grief but also serves as a record of your progress as you go through the grieving process. You can reflect on how your perspective on the loss has evolved over time to realize how your mourning is a continuous process.

3. Using your creativity

Making art, crafts, and music are all methods to use your creativity and deal with intense emotions.

4. Making time for grieving

Although scheduling mourning may seem paradoxical, scheduling a set period of time each day for grieving might aid in the full processing of strong emotions. Find a place where you feel comfortable letting yourself grieve without worrying about others' opinions. During that time, give yourself the freedom to cry, yell, or otherwise express intense emotions.

5. Refrain from making significant changes in your life

A significant loss can cause a lot of disruption in your life, so it's important to maintain as much of your current routine as you can. Wait until you have dealt with the grieving process for a while before making significant life decisions, such as changing employment, moving, or anything else.

6. Regular exercise

Include physical activity in your schedule to help you let go of stress as a way to express your grief. If you want to release your rage and frustration over your loss, you can punch and kick a punching bag or go for a peaceful run or walk to calm your body and emotions.

7. Engaging in social activities

Spending time with friends or joining a social group will help you avoid being isolated at home where your grief may consume you.

8. Reminiscing in a healthy manner

Your pleasant memories of the deceased person might be consoling during mourning. Take some time to browse through old photos, read words left by the deceased, or view movies that were shot during the life of your loved one. Additionally, you can find it beneficial to speak out loud to or write to the deceased in order to express your sentiments to them and keep a connection that endures even after death.

9. Pay tribute to your loved one

Consider volunteering or making a donation in honor of the deceased if they had a passion for a certain cause or organization.

Spending time with pets can help you deal with sadness since they offer unconditional affection and comfort. Consider volunteering at a nearby dog shelter to walk the dogs or socialize puppies so they are prepared for adoption if you don't have any pets of your own.

10. Participating in a grieving support group

Being in the company of people who have also just suffered a significant loss can ease your load of grief. There may be a local support group for those who have lost someone to a certain ailment, such as cancer or heart disease, if your loved one passed away from it.

However, in the early stages of the raw grief phase, even seemingly insignificant issues may be too much to handle.

Unhealthy ways to deal with Grief

People frequently mention employing different coping mechanisms at this point as well.

Unhealthy coping techniques could be:

1. Denial: refusing to express your sorrow or loss.
2. Taking unnecessary risks, such as acting without considering the repercussions or venting frustration in unhealthful relationships.
3. Substance abuse involves using drugs or alcohol to dull your feelings.
4. Overeating or undereating: utilizing food as a sedative or diversion.
5. Obsessive/controlling behavior: since your loss was beyond your control, you might try to control what you can.

Unhealthy coping techniques can result from a variety of circumstances, such as low self-esteem or a history of untreated anxiety and depression. Their loss may feel intolerable due to a sense of emptiness or a lack of safety, and this inability to handle the emotions causes them to engage in those undesirable behaviors.

Chapter 5:

Navigating Practical Tasks and Responsibilities After the Loss of a Spouse

Managing finances and legal matters

Losing a spouse can cause difficult financial and legal issues in addition to grief. It can feel overwhelming to adapt to a new situation, but it can be done with care and planning.

The greatest stressor a person can experience, according to the Holmes-Rahe stress assessment, is losing a spouse. Uncertainty and emotion are present, without a doubt. Even though it's probably the last thing on your mind right now, it's crucial to properly analyze your financial condition. Avoiding rash financial decisions during this emotionally charged period is essential to ensuring that your finances are optimal and that you may successfully continue down your chosen life path.

It is crucial to discuss your situation with your financial advisor in order to identify the various impacting variables that are affecting it and determine how they might be addressed. Do you have any children who are dependent on you? Do you have a job? Have you established an emergency fund? How you handle this life event will be impacted by a number of factors. You don't yet have a mentor? Finding a fiduciary financial advisor now would be excellent.

Through these difficult transitions, a fiduciary can be a valuable copilot, and you receive legal protection because the fiduciary is obligated by law to act in your best interest.

Here, we'll go through a few actions you may take after losing a spouse to make sure you come out of this turmoil with stability and a well-thought-out plan.

1. Do not act rashly.

There is no disputing that losing a spouse is a tough and painful moment, and given the emotions involved, it can be difficult to maintain your focus in order to make timely and responsible decisions.

Selling your home to move closer to friends or family or choosing to assist other family members with significant bills before fully understanding your financial status are all examples of major decisions that should never be made under stress. You require a route. To make choices that will affect your security and pleasure over the long run, you must have a complete understanding of your financial circumstances. The ideal situation is that you and your fiduciary financial advisor have had time to examine the fundamentals of this circumstance and have a plan in place, regardless of whether the timing of this loss was partly predicted or an outright surprise.

2. Track Down Vital Documents

It's reasonable that you might not have all of your crucial financial and legal paperwork organized and in their proper locations at the time. It's alright. But you must take care of this procedure as soon as you can.

obtaining, identifying, and arranging important documents such as marriage and death certificates, bank statements, insurance policies, social security numbers, pension information, and information about

401(k)s. Ideally, you had your files organized before this, whether you stored them with your adviser for quick access or organized your data in paper form or online, but if not, get to work as soon as you can.

3. Begin to Construct Your Plan

Check your paperwork to see if there are any that relate to your life before your spouse's passing as well as your life after. As you navigate the estate settlement, the records that pertain to your life before losing your spouse will be crucial. To assess your demands as they are right now, those that are relevant to your current circumstance will be crucial. What should your spending plan be? What will your monthly social security benefit be? Is the benefit from your spouse's life insurance policy sufficient to pay your current expenses? Here, we'll get right to the point and determine what you already have and what you'll need in order to proceed.

Debts that existed before the death of your spouse will be examined and dealt with. Of course, you're accountable for your own personal commitments, but what about your spouse's? Usually, the deceased person's "estate," or the possessions and funds they leave behind, is used to pay off debts. Finding out your state's rules and what you are accountable for is crucial because if you reside in a community property state, you may be held responsible for your spouse's debts even though you did not sign them. Arizona, California, Idaho, Louisiana, Nevada, New Mexico, Texas, Washington, and Wisconsin are states that have community property laws.

4. Get organized

- Begin with the fundamentals. Focus on developing a thorough understanding of your assets, liabilities, and cash flow in the near future. Throughout the first few months, keep a journal of your money interactions and conversations.

- Obtain copies of death certificates. Ask your funeral director or doctor for 10 to 15 copies of the death certificate. For prospective changes and modifications to financial, legal, and estate planning documents, several copies will be required.

- Discuss estate planning. Most likely, you received a sizable inheritance from your spouse's property. assemble the necessary estate planning papers, including a trust or a will.

- Speak with credit bureaus. Inform Equifax, Experian, or TransUnion about your spouse's passing, and terminate any accounts kept in their name. To check for any unforeseen debt, you might also wish to acquire a copy of your spouse's credit report.

- Remember to include your spouse's digital assets. These procedures can let you access their digital assets even if you don't have their usernames and passwords for online accounts saved in a safe place or using password management software like LastPass.

- Meet with reliable counsel. Before making any changes to accounts or exercising beneficiary or death claims, consult with your financial counselor, tax advisor, and/or attorney. They might have choices that could benefit you when claiming assets from a tax standpoint that you are unaware of.

5. **Examine how you're doing financially right now.**

- Determine your overall assets. Don't forget to account for your checking, savings, and investment accounts, as well as your house, car, and any other real estate or property you may own.

Subtract any current liabilities, such as mortgages, vehicle loans, credit card balances, and other debts. You can control this process with the aid of a financial expert.

- Revise account titles. Modify any joint titles you may have, including those for your home, car, investment, and credit accounts. Bank accounts are one exception; think about keeping your spouse's name on the account for at least six months in case any checks arrive.

- Investment accounts that roll over or transition. If you are the named beneficiary, your spouse's qualified accounts, including any 401(k)s or IRAs, may be transferred to and rolled over into your qualified accounts. There may be more choices, such as setting up an inherited IRA.

- Bear in mind taxes. In the year of your spouse's passing, you must file taxes on their behalf.

· Exercise caution before selling. Even though you might think about selling your house, make sure to exercise caution at the beginning of the process. You and your family may experience additional emotional strain as a result of moving away from home. Refrain from wanting to pay off your mortgage as soon as possible. In the short term, having enough cash on hand is probably much more crucial for your long-term financial stability.

6. Factor in insurance

- Speak with your partner's employer. Contact the human resources office to settle the current policies and receive benefits if your spouse's employer offered health insurance or life insurance benefits for your family.

- Speak with insurance providers. If there are any death benefits for beneficiaries, discuss these with your insurance agents.

7. Recognize third-party advantages

- The Social Security Administration should be informed. When you begin getting your benefits has both benefits and drawbacks. For example, if you're the widow of a spouse who worked overtime enough to apply for Social Security benefits, you can begin collecting the entire survivor benefit as early as age 60 (age 50 if you're handicapped). This is known as your "full retirement age." If you accept your benefits early, they will be decreased, but they may also give you the cash flow you require. If you are taking care of young children, you can potentially be eligible for benefits.

If relevant, look into veteran's benefits. Information on services and benefits available to spouses is available through the Veterans Benefits Administration.

8. Enlist Some Professional Help

While your friends and family will be an invaluable source of support at this time, it's critical that you seek advice on critical choices from a dispassionate expert who has the requisite experience to help you through this shift in your life. At the very least, get in touch with your advisor (or find one) and ask for assistance in creating a plan and getting in touch with other experts as necessary, such as:

- The HR Department of any former employer or business where your spouse worked in order to access any potential benefits;
- An attorney to assist you with the will or any trusts.

- The Social Security Administration, or if your spouse was a veteran, the Veteran's administration to assess advantages.

- Insurance agent to find out whether your husband may have had any insurance. Ideally, your financial advisor already has a copy of this. To find out what assets you have in separate or joint accounts, as well as any safe deposit boxes, contact your bank or banks.

Unquestionably, one of the biggest challenges in life is going through the terrible loss of a spouse. It does not, however, imply that you are unable to go on and lead a fulfilling life. It's crucial to keep in mind to take care of yourself by maintaining healthy food, exercise, and social connection. After such a tragedy, managing your finances will give you the stability and freedom to embark on new activities and create a satisfying life.

Making Decisions about shared property and possessions

Many women are unsure of their rights to their husbands' possessions. Following her husband's passing, a wife's rights to his property are based on:

- Joint ownership between a husband and wife.
- The husband's property's type—self-acquired or inherited

Joint ownership

When a husband and wife jointly acquire property during a marriage, the kind of ownership determines the wife's rights to the property following the husband's passing. The co-ownership may consist of:

1. Tenancy in Common

No right of survivorship exists. When a co-owner passes away, his share is divided among his legal heirs.

2. Joint Tenancy

The remaining co-owners inherit the deceased co-portion owner's of the property.

3. Tenancy by entirety

A unique type of joint tenancy known as tenancy by totality only occurs between husband and wife. In this type of ownership, neither spouse may transfer their portion of the property to a third party without the approval of the other owners. This lease may be canceled by mutual consent, a divorce, or the passing of either spouse.

4. Presumption of Ownership

The law presumes tenancy in common between the co-owners unless otherwise specified in the deed. The assumption is for tenancy by the entirety in the event of a married couple, unless the deed provides otherwise.

To prevent legal issues later, it is always advisable to disclose the kind of ownership in the title deed.

Distribution of property to wife and other legal heirs:

A. If the joint ownership is –

- "Tenancy by the entirety or joint tenancy with survivorship" - in this case, the property passes to the wife upon the death of the husband.
- "Tenancy in Common" - under this arrangement, the husband's legitimate heirs become joint owners and their

portion of the property passes to them in accordance with the applicable requirements of the Hindu Succession Act, personal laws, or India Succession Act.

B. In the case of joint property of husband and wife: If the fact is established that

- The property is purchased by the husband but is held in joint names; as per the applicable law, the wife is one of the legal heirs to the full property.

- The property is held in joint names and was bought by the wife alone with her wages; she is the only owner of the entire property.

When a husband and wife purchase property jointly and both make contributions to the purchase, the property is divided according to the contributions made, and from the husband's portion, the wife receives her share as a legal successor under the applicable legislation.

Self-acquired and ancestral property:

1. Under Hindu Law

If the husband passes away intestate, the wife only has the right to inherit the property after his passing. The Hindu Succession Act, of 1956 lists the legal heirs of a male who passes away intestate, and the wife is listed as a Class I heir and receives an equal share of the estate as the other legal heirs.

If the property is:

Self-acquired: The woman inherits as a Class I heir if the husband passes away intestate.

Ancestral - The wife has the right to receive a portion of the property owned by her husband, but she is not allowed to divide. In the event that the division of the ancestral property is impacted, she receives her portion as a class I legal heir.

For those of other faiths besides Hindus, the transfer of property is governed by personal laws or The Indian Succession Act.

- For Christians, the property is regarded to have been gained by the widow independently of the deceased husband's legal heirs, regardless of how it was acquired.

- Muslim law also recognizes the wife's entitlement to her deceased husband's property, which is typically one-fourth if there are no children and one-eighth if there are.

Adjusting to a new routine and living situation

After your husband passes away, how do you live alone? Remember that you are not alone right away. The helpful advice and suggestions in this section may enable you to proceed, but the feedback from readers in the section below is comforting nonetheless. In the company of other widows, you'll discover more support and hope for living alone after your husband's passing than in any blog post or book. Please take the time to read their tales and comments.

Future planning can be frightening and intimidating. Try to keep your attention on today rather than getting too far ahead of yourself. What obligations do you have today? How can you treat yourself gently and kindly? That would be a wonderful place to begin.

Ideas for a Life Without Your Husband After His Death

These practical suggestions for living alone after losing a partner won't apply to everyone. Nothing functions for everybody! These are merely recommendations from other widows who have dealt with the loss of their husbands; they might not be appropriate for you, but I hope they will at least make you feel less alone.

1. Be patient with yourself and kind to yourself.

Many wives rely on their husbands to handle the finances, the automobile, and even the yard. When the dishwasher malfunctions, the trees need pruning, or the automobile needs snow tires, husbands are frequently the "go-to people." I rely on my spouse to take care of our retirement savings as well as the bills and taxes. I'm aware that this is a mistake and that I might later regret not getting more involved in our financial concerns. I have faith in my spouse and know he is handling our finances responsibly, but I should know more than I do.

Certain household duties and financial obligations may make you feel helpless and despairing.

Because of how little you understand about your portfolio, retirement fund, taxes, and other financial matters, you can even feel humiliated. Learning all of this is a difficult task, particularly when you're getting used to living alone after your husband passes away. You experience exhaustion, loneliness, and overwhelming grief. Slow down and be gentle with yourself. Reach out and request the assistance you require.

2. Think about bringing fresh energy into your house.

Some widows claim that having a cat or dog to look after makes living alone after their husband's passing easier.

A dog or even a kitten can motivate a person to get out of bed and venture outside in addition to providing companionship. Cats and dogs can be friends for ladies who aren't accustomed to living alone and can add life and presence to an empty home.

Walking your dog will motivate you to socialize with your neighbors, get some fresh air, and exercise. Walking a dog has positive emotional and physical health effects, such as boosting mood, increasing appetite, and reducing feelings of loneliness.

3. **Consult with family and friends about finding a roommate or tenant.**

I value my privacy and space, so this would not be my first choice for adjusting to life without my partner.

I'm an introverted writer who enjoys spending time alone. However, many women find that following their husband's passing, their homes are too quiet and empty. The loneliness is too great, and the silence is deafening. You can cover the void and get used to life without your partner by finding a housemate or tenant.

Before your husband passed away, were you socially active? Living alone might be much more challenging for you. Perhaps you're an extrovert who enjoys company and conversation. A short-term renting arrangement can help you deal with living alone after the loss of a spouse, much way fostering or adopting a pet can.

Here are a few simple suggestions for adjusting to living alone after your husband passes away:

- Sort through your basement and attic, clean out your closets, and declutter your house. Recruit a friend to assist you.
- Reposition the furnishings in your bedroom and living room. This may serve as a reminder that times have changed and aid in your adjustment.
- Add some light to the shadowy nooks and crannies; white twinkle lights are a lovely addition to any home's illumination.

- Steer clear of watching the news or other upsetting or depressing programs.

- Pay attention to what makes you feel low and drains your vitality. Do less of it, even if it means spending less time with loved ones you once had close relationships with.

- Talk to people who share your interests. It's necessary to reach out to others in order to receive the support and hope you require; nevertheless, you are not required to join a grief support group for widows.

Chapter 6:

Finding Meaning and Purpose After

the Loss

Living through grief is one thing, and living past it is another. The loss of a spouse is enough to completely change someone's life, sometimes temporarily and other times, permanently. But what happens when you have grief in check? What comes next, when you feel like you're already recovering from the pain and sorrow that came with the loss?

I say it's the best time to get your life back on track and make new meaning to it again. This chapter looks at how you can rediscover purpose, which is one great step to living life to the fullest.

Exploring new passions and interests

It is undeniable that not everyone is as fortunate in finding their passions. Some individuals have said that you either have it or you don't, in my experience. But I don't believe that to be the case. Finding your passion can be challenging at times, but there are techniques to make yourself more receptive to doing so.

1. Learn a Skill

Most passions begin with learning new abilities. Marathon runners, musicians, and other creatives all learned their craft at some point in their lives and modified it. Learning new skills is great since you may practice them for a few days to gain a feel for them. Find out if it's right for you by enrolling in a few lessons.

2. Explore

Finding your passion in life may require taking a new perspective on the surroundings. Travel can give you a new perspective on life and motivate you to do incredible things.

Traveling isn't the only option, though. Wander around a neighboring park or practice meditation. Whatever will put you in an introspective frame of mind will be effective. You will become more focused on your priorities as a result.

3. Stop with things you lack passion for

You won't discover your passion if you spend most of your day playing video games or watching television. Eliminate the distractions from your life, and you'll have more time to devote to the things that are really important. Eliminating the things you don't care about will leave a time gap in your life that has to be filled. I hope you'll fill it with things you're enthusiastic about.

4. Find out who you are

Finding new passions will be simpler if you are aware of the type of person you are. Some people are more adept at manual labor, while others are more creative. That ought to provide you with some direction for finding your passions. I would try anything if you're unsure about this. You'll discover what you enjoy eventually.

5. Hang around passionate folk

People with passion have a lot of energy and enthusiasm. These traits are contagious, so if you're around passionate people, you'll catch their zeal for living. Their actions could provide you with ideas and inspiration for things you desire to undertake. They can also open your eyes to how you might find your passion by sharing insights on how they found theirs.

6. Previous hobbies

Looking into your past is frequently the best place to start when looking for new passions. I rediscovered a passion I had had in this way. I regularly lifted weights while I was in college. I like it, but I quit doing it soon after I graduated. I started doing it again a few years later, and this time it really took over my life.

7. Use Imagination

Loss of creativity is one of the negative consequences of growing up. I can recall a time when I utilized my imagination to conjure up all sorts of bizarre concepts and tales. I would use these concepts to create fantastical artwork or stories. I needed a way to relax because I had so much going on.

Imagination is a potent tool for boosting creativity. It teaches you new perspectives on the world, which is crucial for many ardent endeavors. Innovation leads to creativity, and creativity leads to imagination. If you let your thoughts roam for a bit, you might be startled by the wild and imaginative things you think of.

8. Listen to your Thoughts

When you let your mind roam, where do your thoughts go? Your mind may be trying to inform you that you're interested in accomplishing something if you find yourself thinking about it. Years ago, I used to picture rock climbing when I daydreamed about things I wanted to do before I died. I finally had the nerve to give it a shot. Since then, I've been in love with it.

9. Step outside of your comfort zone

It takes trying new things you might not be excellent at or are frightened to try in order to find things you're enthusiastic about. Even if it doesn't become a passion, it will still be worthwhile to attempt. For instance, after wishing to paint landscapes for a while, I finally gave it a go. Even though the painting wasn't my passion, I'm glad I tried it. I now see that my interests lie elsewhere.

10. Break out from your rut

You probably follow a daily schedule if you're like most individuals. Routines are beneficial for ensuring that your day works smoothly, but they are detrimental to exposing you to novel experiences. Any alteration you can make to your routine will aid in your new learning. The smallest adjustments can occasionally have the biggest impact. But here's the thing; this loss has already altered your routine.

Routines pose a risk when you start operating "auto-pilot." Have you ever been driving down the road and forgotten the last few minutes, but you managed to make all the turns? A regimen can change your life in that way.

11. Make new friends

Your environment is changed by the personalities of new people. They have unique tastes and dislikes as well as perspectives on the world that you might not have previously considered. Someone will eventually expose you to a new passion.

Additionally, if you frequently mingle with new people. You'll be prompted to introduce yourself. You'll feel more pressure to find that passion in your life if you go too long without coming up with anything.

Meeting New People

At this stage in your recovery, it is not too early to start picking up new hobbies and meeting new people, and I offer you a way to achieve both. We've already established that surrounding yourself with lively and loving people will greatly help you recover, so meeting new people doesn't just have to be about finding a new partner.

Finding enjoyable activities to perform in your spare time is the goal of having a hobby. Everyone should have one or more enjoyable hobbies, but far too many individuals don't find the time. A new pastime might be a fantastic way to make new acquaintances if you don't have many. A fantastic approach to feeling alive again after grieving is to pick up a new interest, and internet therapy can also help you rekindle your passion in other ways. Women can connect with people through a variety of interests. Let's examine a few of these pastime suggestions.

How To Meet New People Or Find Hobbies

Join a book club.

These days, book clubs are extremely popular. They can be fantastic for pretty much anyone who enjoys reading. It's a smart pastime that might offer them a fresh source of reading content they hadn't before considered. It can also introduce a sizable (or small) group of readers and provide them with a topic of conversation. Even if all the conversations revolve around reading, it's still a terrific way to stand apart. Additionally, it may result in coffee dates and chances for gatherings outside of the book club. It will be a way to learn something new, get out of the house, and engage in something that everyone can enjoy, even if it is merely a method to discuss new books. A book club can be the best option if reading is one of your current favorite pastimes.

Become a member of a volunteer group

There are numerous volunteer organizations that engage in a diverse range of endeavors. Anyone seeking to join one of these groups can do so without a doubt, and they can discover a cause in which they firmly believe. You might look for a group that concentrates on assisting women if you're seeking new hobbies for women in particular. Participating in a volunteer group can be a fantastic hobby and is crucial for the neighborhood and the entire planet. This is a fantastic way to get involved if you want to but can't provide money. You may help while still saving money by volunteering, which usually just takes a few hours and is completely free. Participating allows you to give back and meet new individuals. It's the ideal pastime for someone who values helping others and is outgoing.

Enroll in Dance Classes

Women who want an energetic or creative hobby might consider dancing of all genres. Ballet, jazz, tap, belly dancing, line dancing, or any other form you prefer may be covered in dance classes. If you enjoy getting to know the person sitting next to you, partner dances like bachata, salsa, or the tango are terrific hobbies. Who knows, you two might make a good dance team! Dancing takes many different forms because it is practiced all over the world. And everyone, regardless of age, can learn a new style of dance in their spare time. The trick is to go out and enjoy yourself. Everyone in the class can laugh at themselves and each other when that is taking place. People will undoubtedly feel much closer to one another while they are laughing together, and this will have a significant impact on how quickly everyone forms friendships.

Join a team in a sport

Tennis, volleyball, baseball, soccer, and football teams are all offered for a variety of age levels. For ladies who are athletic or simply want to get more fit while having fun, they make great hobbies. Almost all sports have adult leagues available, and women can participate in coed or women's sports. In either case, playing the game fosters a sense of camaraderie among all of the teams and undoubtedly strengthens relationships. Overall, it's a fantastic pastime that may foster a spirit that extends beyond the playing field. Subgroups for various running speeds are typically included in running groups. However, the group will probably assemble at the end for refreshments or conversation.

Be a part of a business organization

Women's hobbies may concentrate on professional objectives. A business association is a grouping of people with a common interest in one or more company kinds or fields. This enables like-minded individuals in similar situations in their businesses or working toward comparable goals to converse and collaborate. They could entail making speeches, attending special events, and listening to speakers. For someone who is driven and enthusiastic about the business, it's a terrific pastime. Although it may begin as a chance for networking, it might develop into friendships.

Enroll in a fitness class

For ladies who wish to stay in shape while interacting with others, there are pastimes as well. Exercise courses are a fantastic method to improve physical and mental health. They can also be enjoyable. Dance lessons can be a fun way to exercise. Yoga, spin classes, Zumba, and a ton more are also offered. Gyms and personal trainers offer standard exercise programs. Additionally, it's a terrific approach to guarantee that everyone benefits the most from the experience.

Join a Bicycle Club

Anyone may have a great time biking, and these clubs occasionally allow families to join.

Female pastimes don't have to be done alone. This implies that a single parent or someone with a family could bring everyone along for the bike trips. It might serve as a means of establishing family ties for these people. For those that join more specialized riding clubs, it can be a chance to engage in a good workout, lower stress, make new friends, and discover the neighborhood where you live. It all comes down to working hard and obtaining a fantastic reward.

Play online games

Meeting people from all over the world can be done through online gaming. While some games need an online purchase, others allow free registration. Although connections formed in this method might not be exactly like those formed in person, they are still a terrific option because they are more diverse. People typically associate video game culture with internet gaming. Card games and even online board game variants are among the numerous additional alternatives. Participants in these worlds can interact with people from all origins and cultures. Despite the fact that males predominately play online games, more and more women are getting involved since they make great pastimes. You can play online games and converse with other players while maintaining more friendships and having fun doing what you enjoy.

These can still be friendships that go beyond the video game platform, even though there won't likely be any face-to-face meetups.

Take Up Choral Music

A great activity for someone who has always thought about singing but hasn't had the perfect outlet is joining a choir or chorus. They do in fact exist in numerous locations, and anyone can participate in them. Even better, participants can range in vocal ability from excellent to merely passable. To have fun and socialize, they can join a chorus. It's a fantastic method to enjoy some excellent music and really improve the neighborhood.   This is particularly true given that the majority of choirs will perform at various local events.

Take Up Amateur Theatre

Women can engage in acting as a hobby. Most localities have amateur theaters, which give those who have never participated in theater the chance to truly get in and try something new. There are roles for both inexperienced and seasoned workers, and there are many paths one can take to succeed in the position. Even helping out on the crew that works in the background may be entertaining and a great way to meet new people.

A spoken word group can be interesting if you're looking for something a little different than conventional theater. The important thing is to experiment and attempt new things, which will happen at every step.

Enroll in a cooking course

People of different ages and culinary backgrounds can engage in cooking classes. Additionally, it teaches a fundamental skill that anybody can employ. Whether the program necessitates partnering up

78

or not, cooking is a terrific opportunity to meet new people and get to know them while everyone is working on that amazing new recipe. Being able to cook will undoubtedly increase anyone's level of independence.

These classes can end up being fantastic opportunities to meet new people with a little bit of thinking outside the box.

One could attend a wine class in addition to cooking classes. Find out whether your neighborhood wine shop offers any classes or wine tastings. You could discover your favorite wine varieties or how to pair wines with different foods. Another excellent method to bring a group together and get them chatting is through wine tasting.

Take an art course

Women who enjoy art might engage in a variety of hobbies. There are many art classes available, and they can focus on many forms of art.

People can participate in a variety of popular art forms, such as ceramics, sculpture, painting, and sketching, and these activities frequently promote teamwork. As a result, those who take part might broaden their skill set and get to meet other artists or art enthusiasts. Anybody can have a lot of fun with this, regardless of their level of expertise. Try going museum hopping one day if you enjoy admiring rather than making art. Many museums also give a free day if you're looking to save money.

Finding ways to honor and remember the person who has passed

You might find yourself wishing to commemorate your husband's birthday in some way even after he passes away. Even though he is no longer a constant in your life, you can still be happy that you had him for the time you did. Birthdays can be a wonderful occasion to honor the traits that made your husband special to you.

1. Host a birthday celebration in memory.

Did your husband enjoy celebrating his birthday with friends and family? If so, a memorial birthday celebration is a wonderful opportunity to pay tribute to him.

Invite everyone he might have invited to a barbecue in the backyard or a dessert gathering while he was alive. You may all come together and converse while having fun.

2. Hold a charity event in his honor.

It might be a wonderful idea to organize a fundraiser in your husband's honor on his birthday if he had a particular cause that was dear to him. People can donate to a certain organization on their late husband's behalf. Even internet fundraisers can be set up to quickly gather support.

3. Enjoy a movie night

Renting his favorite movie helps to keep those memories alive. Use the occasion to spend some quiet time alone reflecting on him, or invite the rest of your family to join you.

If you and your husband shared children, his passing will have an impact on your entire family. Children may find Father's Day particularly difficult since it frequently serves as a sad reminder that they are missing a significant adult in their life. Spend some time preparing a Father's Day tribute for your dad with your kids. It might rekindle their memories of better times.

4. Enjoy some quality time as a family.

If you and your children are no longer able to celebrate Father's Day with their father, you can at least spend the day together. It will be up to you how that time is spent. You might wish to go through old family pictures that you have. Some of your best memories and tales can be accompanied by seeing the images of a deceased loved one.

5. Encourage your children to write their father's letters.

Younger children may frequently feel as though they are missing out on important memories of their deceased parents.

You can encourage them to write a letter to their deceased father on important occasions in which they discuss their current circumstances. It's a beautiful approach to showing respect and can help your kids feel the connection they might be lacking.

6. Engage in a hobby he enjoyed.

Participating in activities that your late husband used to like will help you and your children feel more connected to his memories. It may be a longer excursion like a weekend camping trip, or it might be a quick and straightforward activity like going to the movies. Recreate the experiences you might have otherwise neglected.

Ideas for Honoring a Late Husband on His Death Anniversary

Face the anniversary of a spouse's passing with difficulty. No matter how much time has passed, remembering that date can be upsetting. You can still celebrate the life you used to share on the anniversary of your spouse's passing. These solemn remembrances are a dignified way to honor your partner's memory.

1. Go to his cemetery.

When honoring a spouse on the anniversary of their passing, you don't need to go all out. You might not feel capable of organizing a big event or even just being around people.

The act of visiting a grave is straightforward, and there is a sufficient ritual to give the gesture significance. If you want to make the event a little more formal, you can bring flowers or other cemetery decorations.

2. Compose a letter to him.

You have to acknowledge the day your husband passed away each year while continuing to live without him. It's beneficial to take some time each year to reflect on your progress and major accomplishments. Maintaining your focus by writing letters on your progress is both a simple ceremonial exercise and a way to stay on track.

3. View home movies.

Some family members prefer to concentrate on remembering their husband's life on the anniversary of their passing. A terrific technique to recall your husband when he was content and at ease is to watch films.

No matter how many people are gathered around the Christmas tree or the dinner table, some absences might be difficult to ignore. A lovely approach to honor a spouse who has passed away is to include their memory in your holiday customs.

4. Hang a tree decoration in memory of the deceased.

Together, many families and couples enjoy putting up the Christmas tree.

A wonderful approach to keep your late husband in this tradition is to purchase a particular memorial ornament in his honor. You may either do something more symbolic or have his name etched on an ornament. For instance, if your husband played the guitar, you could purchase a gift in the shape of a guitar.

5. Assign him a seat at the table.

Did your hubby always occupy the same chair? If that's the case, you could be inclined to omit a place setting. However, setting out a plate and some cutlery in advance can be reassuring. Even a small reserved sign can be placed there to signify that you are holding space in your life for him.

6. Prepare his preferred dish or treat.

Food and memories have a close relationship. Eating a portion of food that brings back pleasant memories might actually lift your spirits and help your recollections seem even more vivid.

Ideas for a Memorial or Funeral Service Honoring a Deceased Husband

Immediately following your husband's passing, you can experience extreme confusion. You truly believe that a significant portion of who you are has vanished. You could feel that attending his funeral or memorial service is your final opportunity to honor him. Keep in mind that you will have other opportunities in the future to pay tribute to his memory.

1. Make a speech in remembrance.

People frequently pay tribute to their deceased loved ones during funerals and memorial events. A eulogy is a speech or paper that highlights a deceased person's achievements after their passing. It could be too overwhelming for you to give a eulogy to a close relative like your husband.

But for a lot of people, a spouse really does know best. You are more than welcome to pay tribute to your husband if you feel up to it. You can make this procedure go more smoothly by framing the speech more as a homage than a farewell.

2. Examine memorial poetry.

If you don't have the emotional wherewithal to draft a speech right away after your husband's passing, that is very understandable. You can always read a reading that was written by someone else if you still want to make a statement at his funeral. You can share numerous wonderful works of art created by professional poets and writers during a funeral. Find the funeral poetry that resonates with you; there are already funeral poems for fathers or wives.

3. Create a playlist in tribute.

The music might assist create the right atmosphere for a more laid-back and informal memorial ceremony held at home.

A wonderful way to honor your husband's memory and possibly comfort other visitors is to compile a playlist of his favorite music.

Even after your husband has passed away, honor him

You're fortunate to have a caring partner by your side while you navigate life. Your husband will continue to be a part of your life even after his death. Long after they pass away, the people we love continue to live in our hearts and minds. You can remember the joy your husband brought into your life by honoring him on significant occasions.

Chapter 7:

Dealing with Difficult Emotions

The reality of grief is so much more complex and filled with so many tough emotions and "grief roadblocks" that even the most astute could never foresee.

A "grief roadblock" refers to any of the tough and complicated emotions that stand in the way of our path to healthy grieving. These emotions- like anger, guilt, and regret- are very often responsible for leaving a person in a grief limbo and halting their ability to move forward.

While anger, guilt, and regret are very different emotions, what it takes to move through and push past them is actually quite similar.

Before discussing how to cope with grief roadblocks, it's worth mentioning that all of this is very "normal".

Perhaps not typical for you, and surely not enjoyable or comfortable. However, feeling "stuck" at some point during the grieving process is fairly typical and very normal. Here are some instances of how these feelings could present themselves differently for each person:

ANGER: directed toward the medical community for "missing" something, failing to provide care in a different way, or possibly for failing to provide our loved one with the care we believe they earned. at our friends and family for not being more present or encouraging.

For how they conducted themselves prior to the death of a spouse or for events that have transpired since.

anger directed against the person, condition, substance, or mental illness that claimed our loved one's life. Anger with God, religion, or any other higher force for allowing a bad incident to happen to a good person. Anger at our loved ones for abandoning us.

GUILT: at being unable to do MORE. The "extra" might be anything from pushing our loved ones to take better care of themselves to keep them from leaving the house the night they passed away. guilt about being powerless to stop a drug overdose, suicide, or auto accident... sense that they would still be here if we had just done "more."

REGRET: Not expressing my affection for you more frequently. For not spending more time together or for not always being present for our loved one when we felt we should have been, both physically and mentally.

Honestly, the list is endless. Because these feelings do exactly that— they continue spinning and tumbling us in a cycle that can become so bewildering and jarring that we are unsure of how to break free. There is no moving forward, only looping back, which can leave little faith that anything will change.

Anyone going through this should be questioned about why they allow themselves to get caught in this loop.

Why are you unable to go over these challenging feelings and advance? These feelings are so useless and hollow, and they have no use whatsoever, right?

Wrong.

Since the main surprise is that these emotions DO have a function, once we can identify what that function is, we can break the cycle and start moving on a healthy path.

So what function do they fulfill?

Command.

The knowledge that we have no control is one of the most difficult things to deal with after a loss. Not simply of the life or death of our loved ones, but really of any aspect of life or of what befalls ourselves or others around us on a daily basis.

Can we make an effort to be secure, healthy, and wise in our decisions? Yes, but even when we or a spouse act in the "correct" way, awful things might still occur. It can be quite difficult to accept this. We strive to retain our sense of control so frequently, and it manifests as guilt, rather than giving ourselves over to the really big truth that we have no control over anything in life. I should have taken more action. I might have stopped it. I wish I had been there. We can keep a sense of control over our reality by feeling guilty.

Connection.

There are many things that may be accomplished by ruminating, questioning, and again replaying the occasions leading up to the death of a spouse, but what is the one thing that is most effective? It helps us to remember them. It can be a way to cling on and never let go. demonstrating our inability to forget them, ourselves, and the rest of the world. Additionally, they are with us if we keep them in our minds at all times, even through self-harming and painful thoughts. To always carry them with us is our pledge, our oath, and our goal. even if it causes us to deteriorate and endure pain.

Comfort.

There is a dark comfort in the tangled feelings of mourning, however strange it may appear to someone who has never experienced it. Happiness, joy, and laughter turn into garments that don't fit anymore. And for some people, feeling angry can be more comfortable than feeling sad. Anger has vitality, a goal, and frequently a target. These complex feelings might just as readily serve as deterrents that keep us from facing the true suffering and emptiness we experience, or from experiencing the joy or sense of progress we're afraid to feel.

So, as I so often ask my groups, what comes next? What can we possibly do about any of this if it is true?

Consider the moments when you've experienced a physical issue. a persistent cough, sore throat, or other bodily complaints. We can put up with the suffering for a while, but the cure is in the diagnosis, so a griever's next step is to consider the "why." Why am I retaining these feelings? Starting with a few of the reasons mentioned above, why do I continue to hold on to anger, guilt, or regret if I have decided that I want to and am ready to move forward and I don't want to feel this way anymore?

You alone can provide the solution, so take your time. Write about it in a journal, practice meditation, or consider it while you sleep. Speak to a member of your family or a reliable friend. Even though the reason why isn't always obvious, have trust in the knowledge that it exists and that it holds the key to progress.

It's crucial to choose what comes next once you have determined your personal "why." We can't just declare, "I don't want to feel this way anymore," and then wait for it to happen. This cycle is so established

89

in some people that it is difficult to break. Refocusing our thoughts and energies is what needs to be done.

How to overcome grief's obstacles:

Let Go.

> The first step might be to learn how to let go of the urge to always feel in control of our grieving obstacle that was keeping us from losing control of our lives. One of the hardest things to accomplish is to let go, but with time and effort, we can come to accept the fact that we had no control over what transpired. Take a moment to pause here and consider that. You had no influence over what occurred. I had no control over what happened, tell yourself. Continue doing this until you are free of the weight and burden you have been carrying. By letting go, we can come to the realization that no amount of anxiety, overanalyzing, or second-guessing will ever, ever, ever reverse what has occurred. The only thing we can actually control is this moment—and only this moment.

Construct a Memorial.

The hardest part of grieving is this. How can we proceed without abandoning our loved ones? Is it a betrayal of the loved one I lost if I briefly experience joy? Shouldn't I endure some sort of pain forever to keep them and their memory close to my heart? We can keep our connection with our loved one by constructing a monument, memorial, or ritual in their honor. We can advance while bringing them along with us in a way that is beneficial to both of us. Some people take this to the next level by starting a scholarship fund or participating in a walk or fundraiser for a particular disease or cause. Others go about it in a smaller, more private way, such as by wearing jewelry, making a weekly trip to a cemetery or other particular location, or even just by kissing a spouse's photo before going to sleep. You can pay tribute in whatever way feels right to you; there is no right or wrong way to do it.

Allow your partner to act as your guide.

They would want what from you? What would the person you miss and whose death has made it so difficult for you to move on to the desire you have? This is definitely something that some grievers have heard when a friend has tried to console them by stating, "Your mom wouldn't want you to be miserable," I believe that most people don't always take this statement as seriously as they ought to. They would want what from you? You are aware of the solution. They would console you, offer advice, and implore you to pick up the pieces as best you can and get on with life if they were here and you could talk to them. Turn to your lost loved one and listen to their words. Sit with this rather than dismissing it as an idea. You can hear your loved one's voice and can picture how they would say this to you as you sense their presence. This may be a very difficult task, but it helps us stay connected to the person we lost and accept the counsel we know they would give us.

All of this won't occur overnight. Recognize that we struggle and fumble during the grief process. There is the next phase, even if the grieving process doesn't really finish because we will always miss the people we lost. a step in the direction of recovery, optimism, and yes, even joy. However, we won't get there until we put in the effort to remove the obstacles in our path.

The importance of self-compassion and forgiveness

There isn't a magic pill to make you feel better, and I don't believe that being human should be curable. Everything we feel has a purpose, as well as a specific time and location. It hurt because it was important. Because we have loved, we grieve.

It takes a human to be aware of every season and storm they encounter.

Finding out what keeps you from giving up or going stone-cold through "the worst" is another aspect of this.

Affirmations aren't miraculous either, but they've helped a lot of people, including me, go on and rediscover joy.

When given a chance, affirmations changed my course and motivated me to develop many priceless life qualities, including emotional fortitude, patience, compassion, generosity, and peace. At first, they seemed wishy-washy or too basic to work.

Finding your own "I am" statements can give you the confidence to make positive decisions and can show you new methods to deal with strong emotions. You can use them as a mantra for your life after loss or talk, write, reflect, visualize, or meditate on them.

Affirmations are a creative outlet that can help you deal with your grief and find your new course in life. Your resilience training can include encouraging you to gradually open your heart to the beauty that is still present all around you and to change your viewpoint in order to recognize the goodness in life, which is frequently easier to see for others than for ourselves.

To lay claim to this new life after loss, however, requires a significant investment of time and emotion.

Losing someone or something you love is devastating, and it's nothing an emotional bandage can fix. You cannot pretend it never happened or use a special potion to undo it. It needs your tender attention because it is unfiltered and genuine.

I can confirm that promise is the very last emotion you feel at that time. that you can endure your suffering. that new life will emerge from the ashes of your past. that you are on holy ground: start at the beginning. But it's one of the things I know to be true.

The other day, I sent a reader an email in which I expressed my enjoyment in "bringing the agony of my past into the present, in a way that makes the world around me a more beautiful place."

It wasn't easy for me to live up to that affirmation, but I eventually did. Healing takes time to complete.

It takes all of your strength to go through a day when your sadness is still recent. It takes practice to learn how to transform your suffering into something beneficial for both you and other people. You should not rush it.

Knowing that not all of these grieving affirmations will resonate with you and the stage of sorrow you're in, I'm providing them anyway (but maybe they will). Each of us has a unique history, as well as a unique means of coping with and getting through challenging emotions.

These feelings and thoughts are a continuation of my own journey toward improving rather than becoming bitter. They are fragments of the narrative I'm still developing.

Wherever you are in *your* process, I hope this helps.

Here are a few Grief Affirmations for Feeling and Healing

1. My sadness has taught me to be human rather than flawless, which is what I always thought I wanted to be.
2. I am familiar with sadness, hopelessness, and failure. I am also familiar with bravery, survival, and humanity. My tale offers someone hope (even if that someone is me).
3. Everything I feel, everyone I've ever loved, and every stage of my life can fit in my heart.
4. Their breath merges with mine. My light merges with theirs. I carry their heart in my own. Through me, they continue to live.
5. I'm appreciative of the courage it took to take their soul into this new phase.
6. "If I have to fall, I'll get up every time stronger." (Adapted from Oathbringer by Brandon Sanderson)
7. I gaze compassionately at my suffering. I forgive myself when I reflect back on the past. I patiently examine myself when I do so. I try to find ways to give when I look at the world. I still see you here with me when I think back on the memories I have of you.
8. Even though I may never be the same, what I loved still exists in me.
9. "Life will never be the same, yet it can still be good in certain ways." (I got that from a reader. Brilliant.)

Chapter 8:

Moving forward and rebuilding

your life

After loss and grief, returning to a "new normal" is a struggle wrought with conflicting feelings. Grief is like attempting to complete a 1,000-piece jigsaw puzzle with 500 pieces missing. To put the puzzle together, you must seek out those missing pieces. Sometimes, you might find a piece by chance and advance easily. Other times, you might need to turn your entire house upside down only to find one piece. It's crucial to understand there isn't a single right technique to find all of those lost pieces. In a similar vein, there is no one right method to mourn a loss.

Normalizing Grief

Numerous life circumstances might cause bereavement in addition to the particular mourning process. You are not alone if you believe that grieving only happens when a loved one passes away. Grief is a broad emotion that can be brought on by many things, both good and bad.

The process of recovering after a loss is not covered in a manual. It's crucial to avoid losing sight of your own needs by comparing your particular grieving circumstances to those of others. They are missing components from their puzzle, but you are lacking different pieces! How can you put pieces from one puzzle together to make your own puzzle?

Grief-related challenges on an emotional, mental, bodily, and spiritual level

Grief is complicated and can result in a wide range of challenging situations, much like an elaborate 1,000-piece puzzle. It might feel overpowering and have an effect on all facets of life.

It's critical to understand that every challenge deserves your special attention and commitment to recovery. The experiences that follow can be compared to furniture that must be moved in order to uncover some of those puzzle pieces.

Emotional Difficulties

- Anger and betrayal, whether directed at oneself or others or feeling betrayed by a loved one who has passed away;
- Agitation, irritability, and impatience, make it difficult to relax, feel tranquil, and allow healing to occur at your own pace.
- Numbness and apathy: these emotions may prevent you from feeling emotionally connected to others and from mending.
- Loneliness and emptiness: These feelings can make you feel gloomy about the future.
- Anxiety and fear: These emotions can make you feel as though your safety is in jeopardy.
- Guilt and shame: These emotions can make you feel bad about what you did or didn't do in relation to your loss.
- Not being able to influence your own future and feeling useless, impotent, and helpless.

Mental Difficulties

- Concentration issues.
- Difficulties making decisions and solving problems.

- Concentrating on the loss

- Having low self-esteem and doubting your value

- Self-blame and the belief that the loss was your responsibility.

- A decline in interest in pursuits, connections, or jobs.

- Nightmares and adjustments to sleeping habits.

- Paranoia and the sensation that everyone is watching you and anticipating a specific grieving response.

- Believing that nobody can relate to your suffering.

Physical Difficulties

- Aversion changes and weight fluctuations.

- Weakness and weariness.

- Muscle strain and physical discomfort.

- Feeling as though your heart is beating out of your chest or having a racing heart.

- Functioning is difficult due to headaches.

- Anxiety or stomach upset.

- Immune system weakness and vulnerability to sickness, infections, and illness.

You can be frustrated by all of these obstacles in the way of completing your puzzle. That is true! Grief is complicated, and much needs to be moved around in order to fill in the gaps and complete the picture. There is no guide on how to grieve, and there is no timetable indicating how long it takes. In addition, sadness can strike at any time throughout your life, even after you've dealt with those feelings. There will be happy and unhappy days and peaceful and painful moments. It's crucial to realize that just because negative feelings come up again doesn't mean the healing process has to start anew. Momentary painful emotions can be brought on by memories of former identities, talents, or a sense of normalcy. Your personal new normal will exist.

Coping with Grief

There is no one-size-fits-all method of handling loss, just like there are no two unique experiences alike. You are an individual with needs of your own to find comfort in such a trying moment. Finding your jigsaw pieces will require a different approach than that of others. Learning to cope with loss can help you discover new facets of your personality, such as your strengths, passions, and other traits. You owe it to yourself to mourn and heal in ways that respect your individual needs. Let's examine a few of the many ways you can piece together your life to discover that new normal.

To treat Yourself with Kindness:

- Rather than denying your suffering, acknowledge it.
- Recognize and accept the triggers that can lead to pain recurrence.
- Keep in mind that your experience of grief is personal; do not compare it to others.
- Maintaining contact.
- Talk about your pain with those who can connect to it.
- Give yourself space to process your grief in a secure setting.
- Locate a local or online grieving support group that specializes in the type of loss you have experienced.
- looking after yourself.
- Allocate time to focus on a project and channel creativity.
- Proper nutrition, rest, and exercise to prevent physical and mental exhaustion.

- When you feel too overloaded to be productive, take mental health days.

- Take part in enjoyable hobbies and other activities.

- Discover ways to unwind, whether they involve being in nature, engaging in activities such as hiking or swimming, listening to music, meditating, or taking a hot shower or bath.

- Use activities to process and recover from grief.

- Rituals of affirmation, including writing a letter, song, or poem to the departed and thanking them for their love and support, might help you release pent-up regret.

- Gratitude letters that go over happy moments with your loved one, lessons you're grateful they taught you, and qualities you valued in them. The letter should be finished by stating how you may commemorate the person every day of your life via your actions, feelings, and beliefs.

- Memorial gardens or other lovely objects created in honor of your deceased loved one that brings you comfort.

These are only a few of the many strategies that can assist you in managing the challenging emotions of bereavement. Some of these items might be helpful to you, while others might not. There are probably things that you can use that aren't on the list. Grief, after all, is specific to you! Let this understanding motivate you to find coping mechanisms that work for you. You can locate those missing pieces and put the puzzle together. It might take some time, but that's okay! You have the right to mourn in your own time.

You don't have to solve it by yourself.

The role of goal-setting and planning for the future

Whether you are through a crisis in your life, grieving, or just enjoying the road of life, goal planning is crucial to your well-being.

We gain purpose from our goals. On the path to one's destiny or healing, there are numerous objectives that must be met. Goals can give direction, particularly when life becomes ambiguous.

Goals are the stepping stones on the road to success, whether you are attempting to get through a crisis one day at a time or you have a huge vision for your life, family, business, or ministry.

Setting the Right Kind of Goals is Key

Establishing defined goals and a timeline for each one is necessary for effective goal-setting. When your objectives are vague, it is challenging to picture them. Finding the drive to act is made more challenging by this. Another sign of sadness is a lack of motivation.

According to a study done at the University of Liverpool, people who are clinically depressed have a tendency to set broad goals that are challenging to accomplish. To be joyful would be an example of a universal desire.

Those who were not depressed in the study were more likely to have reachable, concrete goals like "better my five-mile marathon time this summer." The researchers came to the conclusion that depression may be sustained and made worse by having highly general and abstract aims.

Numerous studies demonstrate that those who write down their goals succeed in life more than those who omit this crucial stage.

Some Advice on Goal Setting

1. When writing your goals, make sure they are upbeat, future-oriented statements. Avoid using negative phrases like "stop," "don't," or "no" wherever possible. Instead, concentrate on the constructive action you wish to do.

2. Construct concise, action-oriented goal statements. Pay attention to what you wish "to DO."

3. Specify a time frame in which you want to achieve your objective. It could be on a daily, weekly, monthly, or fixed-date basis.

4. Make a list of everyday tasks you can perform to help you achieve your objective.

5. From whom do you need assistance to reach your objective? Tell them what assistance you require from them.

Additional Advantages of Goal Setting

- Points out areas where you can strengthen your weaknesses.
- When completed, it makes you feel accomplished.
- Enhances confidence and self-worth.
- A crucial step in getting over loss or sadness.
- Thinking back on earlier successes can inspire you to achieve current objectives.
- Makes you prioritize, which reduces distractions.
- Offers a direction to take.
- You become accountable for your own achievement.

Do you Make Any of These Excuses for Not Setting Goals?

Maybe you're resistant to change

You might need to try something novel in order to set goals.

Time limitations

You can be saying "yes" to several things that do not fit your genuine purpose rather than concentrating on a single objective.

Dread of failing

Do you believe failure to achieve your objectives will be met with criticism? (Even by the voice inside your head?) Those who establish ambitious objectives but fall short of them frequently achieve considerably more than those who never do. What if you decided to save $5,000 over the course of the following 12 months? Even if all you manage to save during the following year is $3,500, you will still have made more progress than you would have without a target.

Passivity

This is a conviction that events will unfold as they will. While there will always be aspects of our lives beyond our control, there is evidence that when we focus on a goal and declare it aloud, we start to see the world and the people in it working with us to achieve that objective.

Take some time to consider the reasons why you might be putting off creating goals if you find yourself using any of these justifications. Then determine if or how likely it is that these thoughts will come to pass. Find strategies to counteract the negative thinking that prevents you from establishing realistic objectives for your recovery or achieving your destiny.

Setting Grief Goals

The majority of the time, having goals is beneficial in life as well as in the process of doing and developing goals that assist you in keeping track of your progress and future plans. SMART goals, which stand for Specific, Measurable, Attainable, Realistic, and Time-bound, are goals that are even designated as such.

When helping others through sorrow, some individuals may try to help them set goals, whether they be straightforward ones to get through the day or Smart goals that can assist people to identify their challenges, and benchmarks, and track their progress to see how far they have come. There is nothing wrong with trying anything like that, but according to many grieving individuals, smart goals don't always succeed. They are under extreme pressure to advance too soon. Additionally, they believe that their emotions have a shelf life and that if they still experience melancholy, misery, or despair after six months or so, they are doing something wrong.

Have you established objectives during your grieving process? If the answer is no, please don't stress about any notions that you ought to or might benefit from setting goals for overcoming sadness.

If the answer is yes, what challenges do you face in your quest for goal achievement? Does it have a reassuring or uplifting feeling? Does it seem genuine or beneficial?

Grief is an all-encompassing feeling, so how will you treat yourself if you establish goals but don't reach them? Will you berate yourself and make your already challenging loss-related thoughts and feelings even more difficult?

Will you let yourself off the hook, reconsider, and choose another or more manageable objective?

You can decide whether or not creating objectives during your grieving is a smart idea based on your responses to questions like these. Most grieving individuals like to keep things straightforward. The idea of making objectives may seem overwhelming or scary.

Trust your judgment when deciding whether or not grief-related goals are healthy for you. When making such a choice, trust your soul and your heart. The last thing you want to do is put additional pressure on yourself, become overburdened, and then feel stuck in your grief because everyone's grieving process is different.

Ideally, you now understand your position with regard to making goals while grieving. The section that follows offers three suggestions if you're trying to set some goals relating to your grieving. If grief goals aren't for you, scroll down to the next section to read about a goal-setting alternative that can be very beneficial to you during your grieving process.

In general, goals imply that a conclusion is near. Endings in grief are sometimes associated with "getting through it" or "moving on." To "feel better" is another typical grieving objective.

It would be much simpler to achieve objectives like these if the grieving and healing processes progressed linearly over time. Sadly, grief doesn't operate that way. Nobody's journey through grief can be linear.

However, there are a few things you can concentrate on to assist manage loss and live more harmoniously between the agony of grief and everyday events in order to move forward if you feel lost and need some goals to get you on track.

Establish a Sanctuary

A unique spot in your surroundings might be used to process sadness when you're mourning. This location can be a specific spot inside a room in your house, the entire room, the outside, inside your car, a location in your neighborhood, or even a distant landmark.

However, you don't want it to be too far away. It must be close enough for you to make the time to travel there. In theory, you'll gain from frequent visits there while your grieving is at its most acute. You won't need to spend as much time there as your sadness begins to lessen as you process it.

You decide how to adorn the sanctuary. You can place items that help you feel through the feelings that arise and remind you of your unique loved one, depending on where you are.

Making a sanctuary allows you to spend time there, grieve your loss, and set certain rules so that your mind may begin adjusting to life outside the sanctuary as it moves forward. In essence, you're dosing your sorrow. It's a concentrated period to lament and sorrow. It's also constrained. You have the option of establishing a daily time limit for your time in your sanctuary.

There is a holy time to process grief inside the sanctuary. Life can go on outside the sanctuary. You don't have to suppress or dismiss any waves of sorrow that come your way outside the sanctuary; you can compartmentalize them instead. You can either make a mental note to come back to it later or take a few minutes to feel whatever arises.

Create a List of Your Goals for the Upcoming Year

Make a list of your top five goals for the upcoming year while spending some time at a local café, if you can. Make an effort to exclude your pain from your list.

I understand that you want to feel better and that you want the sadness and pain associated with mourning to go away, but if all of your goals are centered on your grief, you can be training your mind to pay greater attention to the pain of your loss.

At first, you might not know what you want, and you could also want something to remember your loved one by. Any objective, no matter how modest or large, straightforward or complex, may be listed. This has to do with your life and your goals.

It's crucial to limit your list of objectives to five or fewer. When grieving, less is more. Less is more when it comes to effectiveness.

Keeping your list of objectives to five or fewer can help you stay focused and more at ease because grief may easily overwhelm you.

Your grieving process will remain somewhat balanced if you list out five life-focused goals. When you're grieving in your sanctuary or standing in front of your refrigerator and reviewing your list of life objectives, you can occasionally experience a sense of normalcy.

Arrange Rest Periods

You may feel more worn out while you are experiencing grief.

Throughout the grieving process, it is crucial to take time to rest and take care of yourself. You will gain from scheduling time to rest, just as you would from setting aside time to spend in your sanctuary.

It's simple to believe that the busier you are, the less painful your grieving will be. That occasionally holds some truth, but more often than not, it's a coping method that might eventually cause more emotional distress.

If you believe that taking a nap won't assist you since your mind would be preoccupied with nothing except your loss, look for a friend who can help you schedule time for relaxing activities. A wonderful illustration of such an activity is movie night.

It can be calming and restoring to your health and sense of delight to find a friend and see a ridiculous comedy.

Nature hikes, baths, naps, massages, stretching, mindful breathing, and listening to music are further relaxation techniques. There are a ton of other things you may do to feel refreshed. This concise set of suggestions should help you get started taking care of yourself and getting some rest.

You may accomplish a lot more things to aid in the grieving process. It does not ensure that you will get over your loss more quickly. But it does ensure that your sadness will receive greater focus and attention, which does speed up the healing process.

Grief-related goals don't have to be specific or evaluated as success or failure, just like other goals in life. When things cease to feel significant, necessary, or relevant, they might be changed, modified, or even replaced. Grief is a draining but potent emotion that can quickly alter one's perspective on goals. If you decide to make goals for your sorrow, be adaptable and open-minded.

If setting objectives for your grief and loss isn't helping you right now, there is another option that could. It involves making daily goals.

Being intentional enables you to concentrate on how you want to be in the moment, regardless of any form of goal fulfillment. This is how intentions differ from goals. You can make intentions based on your values and what is most important to you.

Moments matter while you're grieving. You can manage more emotions that arise by living in the present. Goals are more concerned with the future than intentions, which are more concerned with the here and now.

Intentions are also carried out every day. As is frequently the case when creating goals, there is less pressure to accomplish something monumental.

In times of loss, it can be simple to judge yourself for feeling stuck and/or not grieving properly if the goal was to feel better but three months later you feel worse.

The experience of grief is not linear. Setting intentions as opposed to goals may prove to be more beneficial. Eliminating self-criticism and self-judgment that may result from thinking that your method of grieving is improper might be helpful.

Because goals are more inward, they might be more helpful to you when you're mourning.

They are founded on how you relate to other people and to yourself. Goals are founded on outside successes. Intentions are by nature more kind, forgiving, caring, and supportive of oneself.

Finding supportive and helpful intentions during a grieving process can be difficult. It could be challenging for you to remember details, organize your thoughts, and come to a sound judgment. Setting boundaries, asking for assistance when necessary, being kind to oneself and others, remaining truthful and forgiving oneself and others are a few examples of intentions for dealing with loss.

Please remember that intentions function best when they are loose and flexible as you consider your grief and what you want in life. Setting expectations for oneself is the last thing you should do. The aftermath of loss brings about a lot of change. Transformation is another thing. If any of your objectives become expectations, you might feel bad about yourself if they're not fulfilled. When sadness brings about additional change, try your best to adjust the sails. Maintaining an intention as an intention is one way to make sure of that.

You should now be able to decide whether creating objectives for your sadness would be more beneficial for you than focusing on particular goals.

Whatever you decide, being kind and compassionate to yourself is essential to your development, healing, and even your impression of feeling better and overcoming grief.

If you have grieving goals, try to keep them straight. If you make plans, be open-minded and adaptable. Grief navigation involves accepting the present and respecting your own thoughts and feelings. Avoid any pressure, whether it comes from within or without. Honor the process' timing and have faith in it.

The importance of self-discovery and personal growth

It promotes healing.

Dealing with the internal problems that prevent you from reaching your full potential is a requirement of being on a personal growth path. In order to process them, let them go, and achieve true inner peace, it urges you to become conscious of your anxieties, emotional discomfort, childhood issues, limiting beliefs, and unhealthy routines. The way to healing is via personal growth.

It makes you feel less isolated.

Continuous self-education allows you to CONNECT with your true self.

You can feel at ease with yourself when you have this connection, and you automatically learn to enjoy your own company and never really feel alone.

Gives life significance.

Everything that transpires to you HAS MEANING once you set out on a road of personal development and determine that everything is intended to teach you something and is an opportunity for you to learn and grow as a person. Everything you go through now becomes a lesson for you rather than just a random occurrence meant to frustrate or complicate you. There is a reason for everything, whether it is via self-love, self-forgiveness, presence, letting go, patience, or any other quality.

It fosters your sense of self-assurance.

Knowing who you are as a result of ongoing self-discovery is the first step in developing self-confidence. Your personal development path teaches you that your individuality is precisely what distinguishes, makes you dynamic, and makes you "excellent." As a result, you begin to love yourself naturally and grow steadily more at ease with and confident in who you are.

It assists you in constructing your own reality.

Your connection to your true self will be facilitated by personal development and self-discovery.

When you're in touch with your inner self, you understand that you're not a victim of your circumstances; rather, you create your own reality. You can change your thoughts, beliefs, behaviors, and general energy to coincide with what you want when you live an empowered life.

These are certainly only a few of the MANY advantages of following a path of personal development.

Self-Discovery

How do you define self-discovery? To me, self-discovery entails more than simply understanding your disposition. Understanding who you are and what your aims and purposes are in life depends greatly on self-discovery. What are your core values? What do you think the world is like to you?

The road to self-discovery is made possible by the sum of all these elements. Don't you want to discover your true identity? Self-discovery is crucial for your personal progress and can help you in many ways, in addition to quelling your curiosity.

Self-discovery resembles a divine quest. You learn more about who you are; the activity itself will assist you in connecting with your intrinsic personality, goals, viewpoint, intentions, temperament, etc. What matters more, though, is what you gain through self-discovery and what its advantages are.

Let's examine Self-significance discoveries and advantages. But first, let's take a quick look at what the self-discovery path should entail.

How Does the Process of Self-Discovery Look?

Everyone's trip is unique since each of us has unique experiences and viewpoints. Here are some actions you can do to start your path to self-discovery:

- Discover who you are by picturing what you genuinely want to be (ideal self).
- Define your values; what is important to you?
- Continue to reflect on your behavior and thoughts (it will give you a clear idea of where you are coming from).
- Consider, assess, and put your abilities to the test.
- Explore your hobbies and desires thoroughly.
- Always have a tendency to want more (try new things, learn something new).
- Regular journaling can be highly beneficial for understanding yourself.

It doesn't have to be a difficult path. Give yourself time, and move slowly. It's not like you can find a good piece of furniture in a matter of days. Put a lot of patience and compassion into the time you spend on yourself.

What Do You Think About Self-Discovery?

Aids You in Discovering Your Purpose

What is the meaning and purpose of my life? is one of the most frightening inquiries. You'll be able to find the solution to this question through self-discovery. This is the reason why it is so crucial to find yourself.

Aids You in Discovering Your Life's Motivation

The continuation of the circle of life depends heavily on motivation. Finding out what truly motivates you will be quite simple for you if you fully understand who you are. Is it a quotation, a song, meditation, or a key person in your life?

Aids in the identification of your needs wants, and desires

Self-discovery is a never-ending journey. Because of their dynamic character, our needs wants, and desires will alter throughout time. Self-discovery is crucial since it will keep you informed about what you truly want right now.

It Aids You In Finding Your Passion

Every one of us has a passion for something. But if we are unaware of what our true passion is, what is the point? Finding yourself actually means figuring out what ignites your passion and what makes you feel alive.

Determining Your Mental Ability

The best thing about self-discovery is that it allows you to fully test your mental fortitude. It will be possible for you to fully comprehend your mental capacity. What are your limits? How far will you go? What is the line that you draw? Etc.

Why Is Self-Discovery Good for You?

- You develop a relationship with yourself. You gain a very, very strong connection with yourself as a result of self-discovery, which is one of its greatest advantages.
- Assists you in recognizing your expectations and comprehending why they are there.

- If you get to know yourself better, you can actually get rid of any bad influences you could have in your life.

- It goes without saying that you'll be much more aware of everything going on in your life if the bad influence is gone.

- Self-discovery is also accountable for lowering the level of stress you might consistently feel.

- The path to mending yourself is also the path to self-discovery.

- Self-discovery will assist you in determining the purpose of life

- You develop a special affinity with yourself as a result of all the work you put into learning about yourself. As a result, you never feel lonely and learn to enjoy your own company.

- It boosts your self-assurance since you are so aware of yourself that nothing can make you feel less confident.

Because each of us has had a different experience, we all interpret and see life differently. Therefore, we must understand our strengths and limitations, as well as our desires, values, and other things. The path to personal development is self-discovery.

Chapter 9:

Finding Hope and Happiness Again

Happiness is always the first thing to do when we are faced with a challenging life situation, like the death of a spouse. We accept the notion that we would never again experience happiness because of the enormity of the issue, or that happiness is something reserved for others.

The worst-case situation is that we feel guilty when we experience a brief delight. We tell ourselves that we no longer deserve to be happy.

In that case, have courage. You can regain your joy. You can laugh once more. Joy is once more accessible. Here are some realities about achieving happiness even in widowhood.

You must decide to be happy once more

The problem is this. It doesn't work like this: the months and years don't merely pass before you wake up one morning with a glimmer of joy in your chest. You must desire happiness once more. You must make another happy decision. This entails repairing the beliefs you have internalized. I no longer deserve to be content. If my husband is unhappy, how can I be? Your discontentment isn't beneficial to anyone. Your spiritual family members want you to be content.

The type of satisfaction you experience differs.

It's conceivable that happiness after loss tastes different. It might be a strong sensation of contentment. It might be quieter and less bubbly.

Perhaps you are feeling more appreciation and thanks for all the blessings in your life and for everything you have learned thus far.

Your personal happiness factors vary

The majority of the people I work with acknowledge that their values have altered as a result of the storm they experienced. What was once significant is no longer so. What did not previously receive their attention has now received it. Things that are unimportant fade away. As priorities change. A new phase that you must learn to navigate is what it means to have a happy and fulfilling life without your loved one.

Acquiring happiness in spite of the loss

Your loss has made you more aware of how fleeting life is, and you are now committed to living it to the fullest. Although your loved one is not present, you are. You take each breath with a brand-new sense of gratitude for the gift of life. You commit to living a life and leaving a legacy that will leave the world bearing witness to your heart.

Leading a life of your choosing

You start to realize that you have a lot of love to give and receive. Although life didn't turn out the way you had hoped, you are still committed to living it on your terms. These ingrained behaviors of living up to other's expectations and adhering to accepted social norms—pleasing others, acting in accordance with others' expectations, and giving till it hurts to give—fall away. You start to consider your values and how you want to live out the rest of your life. Whether it's relocating closer to the beach, having cake for dinner, or painting in the park. This becomes your new compass for navigating life.

The definition of happiness is fluid

Happiness is more about a deep sense of contentment and a calm sense that everything is going well than it is about sudden bursts of delight and highs. You are aware that everyone and everything is temporary because of the severe sadness you have gone through. You may now understand that a day of crying and feeling despair is only a temporary wave. With the knowledge that happiness will return, you accept it and stay with it.

Strategies for cultivating gratitude and positivity

Many of us are considering ways to enhance our lives and become the greatest versions of ourselves as the new year draws near. Building a good mindset is one of the most crucial aspects of personal development. A cheerful outlook can improve our daily life and enable us to face obstacles with grace and resiliency. Here are some methods you might use in the coming year to develop a more optimistic outlook.

Show gratitude

By concentrating on our blessings, we can change our viewpoint from one of negativity to one of gratitude. Make a list of your blessings each day, or consider sending thank-you notes to those who have had a positive influence on your life.

Develop mindfulness

By staying in the present moment rather than concentrating on unpleasant thoughts or experiences, we can better appreciate the goodness and beauty around us. To help you focus on the present, try yoga, meditation, or even just a few deep breaths.

Look after yourself

Putting self-care first is crucial for keeping a good outlook. This can involve practices like getting enough rest, eating healthfully, exercising, and scheduling leisure and downtime.

Set goals

Having specific objectives to strive for can give us a feeling of direction and purpose, which can be inspiring and motivating. Set reasonable objectives and recognize your accomplishments as you move toward them.

Positive Affirmations

Repetition of affirmations, which are positive statements about who we are and how we live, can transform our thoughts and beliefs. Affirmations that speak to you should be written down and repeated to yourself on a regular basis or anytime you feel the need for motivation.

Surround yourself with upbeat individuals

The company we keep can have a significant impact on our mindset. Limit your time with those who are negative or depleting and seek out interactions with those who are positive and supportive.

Always search for the positive

It's not always simple, but finding the bright side of a situation can help us stay optimistic. This doesn't imply disregarding issues or difficulties; rather, it means finding something to be thankful for or taking something away from the situation.

Forgive others

Holding onto grudges or resentment can make us feel sad and promote a pessimistic outlook. Take into account letting go of old grudges and forgiving others and yourself.

Physical activity

Research has shown that exercise has several positive effects on mental health, including enhancing mood and lowering stress. To increase your happiness, schedule some time for exercise, whether it's a challenging workout or a leisurely stroll.

Seek social support

Because social interactions are a natural part of who we are, they can bring us happiness and good feelings. Spend time with friends and family, and don't be hesitant to get help from a professional if you're having trouble with negative ideas or feelings.

Although it takes time and works to develop a positive outlook, doing so may be gratifying and life-changing. Incorporate a few of these tactics into your routine each day in the coming year to discover how they can improve your life.

The importance of self-care in maintaining mental and emotional well-being

Without a doubt, grieving is psychologically, physically, and emotionally taxing, and caring for yourself is the last thing on your mind.

As we examine in this section, even though you might not feel like it, taking care of yourself can be one of the most helpful things you can do while you're grieving or grieving a loss.

What is self-care?

The term "self-care" is broad and can mean different things to different people. Generally speaking, self-care refers to actions taken to improve one's mental, physical, or emotional health. Self-care is not a selfish activity; in fact, it may be crucial to getting through challenging circumstances.

Self-care tips

Allow time for crying

It may seem obvious to allow oneself space for crying, but Erin from Fighting for a Future emphasizes that this is a vital self-care strategy: "During times of loss, make an effort not to repress tears. In fact, there is scientific evidence to back up the advantages of a good cry for relief. Researchers have discovered, according to Dr. Forshee, that "emotional tears," which are distinct from the tears that keep our eyes lubricated or wash out irritants, include hormones linked to stress. Therefore, crying is a very real way to release tension.

There is no set pattern for how everyone feels the loss, which is why practicing self-care and self-compassion is crucial to navigating the various phases of mourning, according to Erin. Grief is an intangible emotion, and I had to remind myself of that. Everyone's perception of it is unique, including our own. When we experience grief, it can feel different every time. Therefore, when I was going through grief, I didn't judge myself; I just accepted and felt my sensations, and I do this because I respect whatever emotion I'm going through. It's possible for two people who have experienced the same loss to respond to it in quite different ways, and worrying that you're grieving incorrectly will make it more difficult for you to move past it.

Do the opposite of what feels natural

Grief comes in waves and stages, despite the fact that everyone experiences it differently, according to Becca from Missing In Sight: It can change at any time. Since no one can predict when grief will hit hardest, the best defense against its devastating consequences is to give yourself acts of self-care that will help you become stronger to ride out the waves. "Sometimes the agony is sharper at some moments more than others. Self-care can even be done in advance to lessen the impact of impending loss. If you take care of yourself when your feelings of sadness are less intense and more manageable, you'll be better able to handle the difficulties that grieving presents when it manifests more strongly.

"Self-care will enable you to be compassionate and nice to yourself while you're going through a tough period. My advice for practicing self-care is to go against your natural inclination. Because grief can sap our will to live, we must fight against our natural inclinations and do what is uncomfortable.

Connect with others

There is no "normal" schedule for grieving and the process can take some time; it cannot be rushed or coerced. However, Becca noted that connecting with others can be a beneficial kind of self-care during a time of loss: "Connect with others. Grief can be a very alone experience that makes you feel as though no one else can possibly comprehend what you are going through. Loneliness can be overcome through socializing and connecting with others. Engage in social interaction and discuss your grief with a friend, relative, or therapist. You can feel connected and relieve any pain you may be feeling by just going to a coffee shop and sitting among strangers.

Recognize and embrace your grief

There is no right or wrong way to grieve, and you could feel a variety of feelings. Grief is a normal reaction to losing a loved one or a pet. According to Margaret from Phantastic Butterfly, grieving is one of the emotions that can have a long-lasting emotional, physical, and mental influence on you: "If left alone with no self-care, it can wreak havoc and leave you severely crippled. Self-care is essential to helping you nourish or refill the emotional, physical, and mental aspects of yourself. It is also essential to helping you go through your grieving process.

The first piece of advice Margaret gave us for practicing self-care was to acknowledge and appreciate the gamut of feelings you are going through: "This may sound obvious, but it's not. When grieving, we frequently smother or suppress our emotions. Instead, we should allow ourselves to completely accept, experience, and move through the emotions we are grieving. Recognizing the sadness, rage, irritation, guilt, or any other feelings connected to our own loss is essential and crucial to the grieving process.

Why is self-care important in grief? ›

Grief may be unfiltered, agonizing, and nasty. It's crucial to take care of yourself when you're grieving. Self-care is an essential component of rehabilitation and helps lessen mental, physical, and spiritual pain. The way that each person deals with sadness and moves through the grieving process differs.

What is self-care in times of grief?

Take up a skill you are skilled at. Even if the result isn't perfect, it's crucial to immerse yourself in your talents and abilities (trouble concentrating and decreased zest are common in grief). Burn aromatherapy candles while enjoying a warm bath with your preferred scents. Put on a cozy blanket.

You can handle it, even when it seems impossible. It won't feel this way forever.

Be kind to yourself... Think in cycles rather than lines. You're not alone. Grief can give rise to meaning. Your feelings are natural.

CONCLUSION

The process of grieving the loss of a spouse can be long and difficult, but it is also an important journey toward healing and rebuilding one's life. We hope that this book has provided you with valuable information and guidance as you navigate this process.

Throughout the book, we've discussed the importance of acknowledging and accepting grief, and the role of cultural and societal expectations in grief. We've also talked about the importance of self-care, finding support from friends and family, and exploring different coping mechanisms. We've also delved into practical matters such as managing finances and legal matters and navigating the adjustment to a new routine and living situation.

In addition, we've discussed the importance of finding meaning and purpose after loss, dealing with difficult emotions, and the possibility of finding joy and happiness again. We also discussed the importance of self-discovery and personal growth as part of the rebuilding process.

Grief is a unique and personal experience, and there is no set timeline for healing. It's important to remember that healing is a journey, not a destination and that each person's journey will be different. It is important to be kind and patient with yourself and to allow yourself the time and space to grieve in the way that feels right for you.

We want to remind you that you are not alone in your journey and that there are many resources available to help you navigate the grieving process. We hope that this book has provided you with valuable information and support as you work to find happiness again, and rebuild your life. Remember, healing takes time, and it is important to be patient with yourself and continue to take care of yourself as you move forward.

REFERENCES

Campbell, K. (2014, June 12). *What to Do With Your Finances After Losing a Spouse*. Yahoo News. Retrieved January 12, 2023, from https://news.yahoo.com/finances-losing-spouse-131712475.html

Dealing With Difficult Emotions (for Teens) - Nemours KidsHealth. (n.d.). Kids Health. Retrieved January 12, 2023, from https://kidshealth.org/en/teens/stressful-feelings.html

Houston, E., & Millacci, T. S. (2019, April 9). *What is Goal Setting and How to Do it Well*. PositivePsychology.com. Retrieved January 12, 2023, from https://positivepsychology.com/goal-setting/

Mourning the Death of a Spouse | National Institute on Aging. (2023, January 6). National Institute on Aging. Retrieved January 12, 2023, from https://www.nia.nih.gov/health/mourning-death-spouse

Postl, E. (n.d.). *Loss of Husband/Wife/Spouse - Help Grieving the Death of a Loved One*. Grief and Sympathy. Retrieved January 12, 2023, from https://www.griefandsympathy.com/lossofhusband.html

Understanding Grief Within a Cultural Context. (n.d.). Cancer.Net. Retrieved January 12, 2023, from https://www.cancer.net/coping-with-cancer/managing-emotions/grief-and-loss/understanding-grief-within-cultural-context

What is grief? (n.d.). Mayo Clinic. Retrieved January 12, 2023, from https://www.mayoclinic.org/patient-visitor-guide/support-groups/what-is-grief

What is Grief? (n.d.). What is Psychology? Retrieved January 12, 2023, from https://www.whatispsychology.net/what-is-grief/

Campbell, K. (2014, June 12). *What to Do With Your Finances After Losing a Spouse*. Yahoo News. Retrieved January 12, 2023, from https://news.yahoo.com/finances-losing-spouse-131712475.html

Dealing With Difficult Emotions (for Teens) - Nemours KidsHealth. (n.d.). Kids Health. Retrieved January 12, 2023, from https://kidshealth.org/en/teens/stressful-feelings.html

Mourning the Death of a Spouse | National Institute on Aging. (2023, January 6). National Institute on Aging. Retrieved January 12, 2023, from https://www.nia.nih.gov/health/mourning-death-spouse

Postl, E. (n.d.). *Loss of Husband/Wife/Spouse - Help Grieving the Death of a Loved One*. Grief and Sympathy. Retrieved January 12, 2023, from https://www.griefandsympathy.com/lossofhusband.html

Understanding Grief Within a Cultural Context. (n.d.). Cancer.Net. Retrieved January 12, 2023, from https://www.cancer.net/coping-with-cancer/managing-emotions/grief-and-loss/understanding-grief-within-cultural-context

What is grief? (n.d.). Mayo Clinic. Retrieved January 12, 2023, from https://www.mayoclinic.org/patient-visitor-guide/support-groups/what-is-grief

What is Grief? (n.d.). What is Psychology? Retrieved January 12, 2023, from https://www.whatispsychology.net/what-is-grief/

Campbell, K. (2014, June 12). *What to Do With Your Finances After Losing a Spouse*. Yahoo News. Retrieved January 12, 2023, from https://news.yahoo.com/finances-losing-spouse-131712475.html

Mourning the Death of a Spouse | National Institute on Aging. (2023, January 6). National Institute on Aging. Retrieved January 12, 2023, from https://www.nia.nih.gov/health/mourning-death-spouse

Postl, E. (n.d.). *Loss of Husband/Wife/Spouse - Help Grieving the Death of a Loved One.* Grief and Sympathy. Retrieved January 12, 2023, from https://www.griefandsympathy.com/lossofhusband.html

Understanding Grief Within a Cultural Context. (n.d.). Cancer.Net. Retrieved January 12, 2023, from https://www.cancer.net/coping-with-cancer/managing-emotions/grief-and-loss/understanding-grief-within-cultural-context

What is grief? (n.d.). Mayo Clinic. Retrieved January 12, 2023, from https://www.mayoclinic.org/patient-visitor-guide/support-groups/what-is-grief

What is Grief? (n.d.). What is Psychology? Retrieved January 12, 2023, from https://www.whatispsychology.net/what-is-grief/

Campbell, K. (2014, June 12). *What to Do With Your Finances After Losing a Spouse.* Yahoo News. Retrieved January 12, 2023, from https://news.yahoo.com/finances-losing-spouse-131712475.html

Mourning the Death of a Spouse | National Institute on Aging. (2023, January 6). National Institute on Aging. Retrieved January 12, 2023, from https://www.nia.nih.gov/health/mourning-death-spouse

Postl, E. (n.d.). *Loss of Husband/Wife/Spouse - Help Grieving the Death of a Loved One.* Grief and Sympathy. Retrieved January 12, 2023, from https://www.griefandsympathy.com/lossofhusband.html

What is grief? (n.d.). Mayo Clinic. Retrieved January 12, 2023, from https://www.mayoclinic.org/patient-visitor-guide/support-groups/what-is-grief

What is Grief? (n.d.). What is Psychology? Retrieved January 12, 2023, from https://www.whatispsychology.net/what-is-grief/

Made in the USA
Middletown, DE
10 April 2023

28549451R00076